Fucking Trans Women

80-Page Giant!!

Issue #0
October 2010

I made "Fucking Trans Women" #0 over the course of a year or so all by myself. It would not have been possible, though, without your support. Finishing this zine in Iowa was hard, and I sincerely appreciate the help of everyone who even asked about the project; your words kept me going.

Thank you to all of you who gave your encouragement, your dollars for paper and glue sticks (I actually did use them for that,) your kind words, your input, your love, your like.

Thank you to everyone who helped me think this project through, from start to finish: Cherry, Molly, Annie, Tom, Julie, Laura E., and everyone else.

Very special thanks to Genne Murphy.

-Mira Bellwether
October 2010

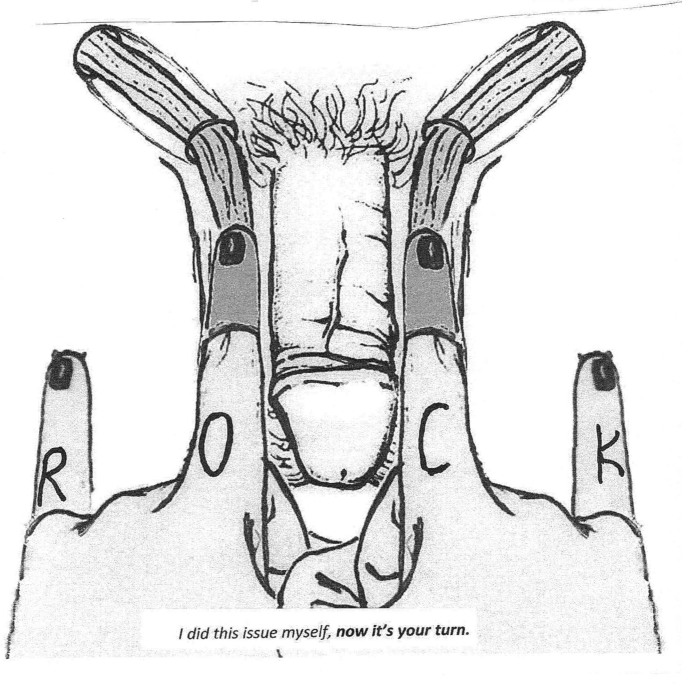

I did this issue myself, **now it's your turn.**

Contents

features

Articles

"Here we were at the beginning or end of the world and I,
            in my sumptuous flesh,
        was in myself the fruit
    of the tree of knowledge;
        knowledge had made me.
    I was a man-made masterpiece
    of skin and bone,
    the technological Eve in person.

I saw myself. I delighted in me."

—Angela Carter, "The Passion of New Eve"

My original motive for starting this zine was simple: I wanted to talk to other trans women about how we like to fuck. Although over the last two years I've found other reasons for making this zine, the overall motive has remained basically the same: to generate conversations about sex with trans women with the knowledge that the more we talk to each other and our lovers about how we like to fuck, the better off we'll all be.

"Why Fucking Trans Women?"

It can be difficult to see certain topics as anything except problems. Most people I've talked to dread the seemingly inevitable difficult conversations with lovers who haven't been with trans women before. Hard subjects come up and sometimes have to be discussed on the spot just as with any sexual relationship. But there's no reason for us to enter these conversations unprepared, nor is there any reason why we can't prep our lovers for these conversations with a little reading material drawn from our own experiences. More than one of my lovers, in fact basically all of them, has at one time or another lamented that there's no "instruction manual" for my body. Even if they haven't put it in those terms they have shared a frustration with frequently lacking the vocabulary, the experience, or the knowledge to be the best lover they can be. I can sympathize. I've had to learn all kinds of stuff about my body on the fly that I would rather *not* have learned the hard way. I've had to invent words, metaphors, and stories, to explain to myself and to others how I think my body works, and what it can do.

There are a few principles at the heart of this zine. One of them is that we benefit from sharing knowledge. Another is that the form of someone's body doesn't necessarily determine what that body means, how it works, or what it can do. That is to say that just because what's in my crotch looks like a penis doesn't necessarily mean that it works like a penis. In point of fact it doesn't, at least not most of the time. I also believe that one of the best tools we have at our disposal for figuring out our bodies, for learning about them and coming to delight in them, is experience. Someone else might say "exploration" or "experimentation" and mean something similar to what I mean. I'm talking about starting from data and working toward conclusions rather than the opposite; something very much like sexy mad science (white lab coats and leather gloves optional.)

I'm talking about beginning with sensation, not with names, vocabulary, or the things we think we know about our bodies. I'm talking about the kind of earnest self-investigation behind using a mirror to look at parts of yourself you couldn't otherwise see. I'm talking about keeping an open mind (and possibly a journal) about your body and considering the distinct possibility that you are looking at uncharted territory.

Here be dragons and sea monsters, my fellow genital cartographers, and we have a lot to learn from poking them. Let the metaphors, the language, the analogies come afterward. They are helpful, but I believe with great conviction that what I have between my legs is not a metaphor or an analogy but something new and wonderful. Best to begin from the beautiful explosive moments of pleasure and discovery, and to let the rest come after.

Since the first call for submissions, since the second call, what has changed? What his this project become? This zine still basically answers the question it originally asked, "How," as in "how do we have sex?" but it is becoming something even more than a how-to guide. It is becoming a kind of cookbook.

The goal of this zine is not to provide an authoritative instruction manual or anything close to a complete understanding of trans women's sexualities. This isn't a definitive "how-to" or an instructable, because there are as many ways to fuck as there are sexual encounters. However, we all know that there are certain patterns that crop up in our sex lives and love lives. We keep notes, even if they are only mental notes, on what works best and what our lovers like and don't like. We owe it to ourselves and to each other to share this information for our mutual benefit. We have to start sharing recipes.

"Fucking Trans Women" is basically a cookbook: a cookbook still in progress, created by you, your friends, and your lovers. The recipes are for good sex, tenderness, better communication, intense pleasure, hot fucking, sharing new ideas, and developing and sharing techniques. The more we all contribute the larger the cookbook grows, and if you don't like the recipes you see there's no pressure to use them. You can start a whole new section; write recipes for desserts rather than soups, so to speak. If you're especially good at sauces (ahem) you might write something about that. If you have something to say about table manners, write about it!

This first issue, the Zero issue, **is your invitation** to send in your recipes. Send in your drawings, your journal entries, your essays, your flowcharts, your Ikea-style wordless instructions, step by step instructions, lists of your favorite ways to fuck, comic strips, *anything*. This is your zine. This is your conversation. Whatever your contribution is, it is important. It is necessary.

One point that came up again and again in surveys, **and in my own head**, was that language was going to be an extremely important ingredient to any good discussion of sex with trans women. I hear this point and feel it deeply. Ultimately there was a choice: what do I call things? You will see how I handled that question in various articles, but for now a bit of forewarning: generally speaking I did pick a word for most things and just rolled with it. The alternative, it seemed to me, was writing a zine that was incomprehensible. You may disagree with that, and if so, I will hear you out. In future issues any number of things may change significantly. But for this issue, I basically tried to pick the word that felt both direct and kind without making the topic incomprehensible. One good example of this is the word "fuck," which two or three people objected to.

We deserve to have sex without it becoming a gender studies class

Do I critically interrogate that word and explicate all of its problematic connotations? **FUCK NO.** This zine isn't "Explaining Trans Women," it's **"Fucking Trans Women."** I have no desire to let the issues covered *in this particular zine* switch tracks and change entirely. The question at hand is what we do and how we do it, not a meta-conversation about conversation. Is there room for gentle and casual tweaking of language? Yes. Is there room for a lecture on terminology? Not really. That conversation can happen *elsewhere*, you can even email me or call me to talk, but it really doesn't need to happen here. At the end of the day you have to pick a word, and that's what I did. "Fuck" is the word I use to talk about fucking.

CONSIDER THIS YOUR TRIGGER WARNING

Some Basic Facts About Penises

The organ that we call the penis on most people assigned male at birth is an interesting and fun piece of biological equipment, or at least it can be. It's easy to feel either confused or intimidated by biological penises: they have a reputation for being incredibly simple organs but also for being dangerous, confusing, messy, and selfish. The truth is that they aren't necessarily any of these things, not even necessarily "a penis" depending on the person and the moment. Most of our preconceptions about them are basically nonsense, and I think this is especially true for penises that belong to trans women. The nature of a penis is defined by how it is used and what we understand it to be. A different take on a penis, a different perspective, can produce a completely different experience.

But personally I don't like to take someone to bed without having at least some idea of what is going to work and what isn't. The trick, I think, is to balance what you've already learned with the usual, expected conversations with lovers about what they want, and what will or won't work for them. In other words, it's nice to have some vocabulary but also to be adaptable and ready to learn as you go. So let's have some facts on the ground, keeping in mind that your mileage may vary. Every body is different and nothing is true for everyone. Still, here are a few very basic but useful things I know about biological penises that can help you get the most out of them, especially if you feel inexperienced. As always, keep your communication lines open before, during, and after sex, and solicit as much feedback as possible. When you want to know how to do something better, ask. When you want someone to change what they are doing, ask.

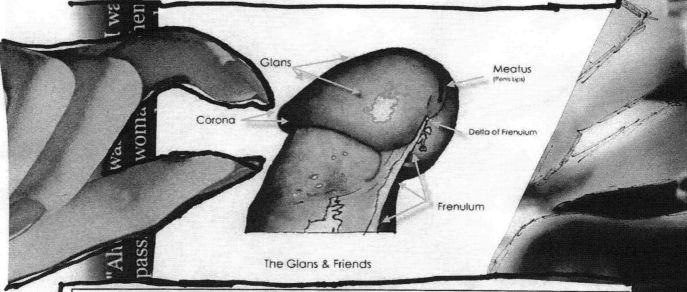

The Glans & Friends

#1: **The most sensitive part is the head.** The glans (head) is the most sensitive part of the penis. It contains the greatest number of nerve endings and these are distributed fairly evenly across its surface. Like the clit many penises have a hood, the foreskin, which protects the head and keeps it moist. Circumcision doesn't affect the sensitivity of the glans directly but circumcised penises do require more lubrication to reach the same level of sensitivity in the glans. Just like the clit, when the glans is properly stimulated it generates an intense amount of sexual pleasure. Stimulation of the glans alone can generate enough pleasure to produce orgasms independently of the rest of the penis. If you want to give someone with a penis a truly memorable orgasm, my advice is to start with the head and stay focused on it. When a penis is receiving pleasure or being pleasured this is almost always where you should concentrate your energy. I think it's often useful to frame penile activities in those terms, the penis receiving pleasure, as a reminder that you're working with an extraordinarily complex, sensitive organ and not just a phallus. Certainly the simplest method of fucking with a penis is "insert and repeat" but that shouldn't be the limit of what we think a penis is capable of.

In general the glans likes gentle-moderate pressure, lubrication, and lots of sensation.

#2: Penises are clits. Structurally, penises are almost identical to clitorises because both develop from the same basic tissues. This is a fairly well-known fact these days but it bears repeating. Both the penis and the clitoris are composed of erectile tissue, both have a head and shaft, and circulation and innervation are more or less the same for both. Contrary to popular belief penises and clits have approximately the same number of nerve endings, although in the clitoris a greater number are concentrated in the head. Sexually speaking the most significant variations between biological clitorises and penises are probably shape and the placement of the urethra. More of the clit extends into the body and more of the penis extends outward; penises generally (but not always) contain the urethra.

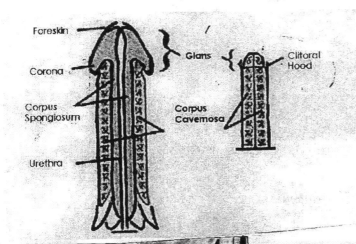

Foreskin
Glans
Clitoral Hood
Corona
Corpus Spongiosum
Corpus Cavernosa
Urethra

If you already have lots of experiences with biological clits but not with penises, try treating penises like large clits, which they basically are.
I dare you.

Some techniques will translate better than others. But the similarities are greater than the differences and even when things don't work you can still laugh and have fun.

#3: Penises are soft. I can't say this enough because it is such an important and frequently ignored fact: most of the time a biological penis is neither rock-hard nor an inflexible rod. They're not supposed to be. The natural, resting state of the penis is soft. Unsolicited erections happen relatively infrequently after the teen years and _____. voluntary boners appear in the dictionary under the entry "diminishing returns."

most penises could never compete with a good dildo on hardness. And those that go the distance are putting themselves at long-term risk: erections that last longer than an hour or so without interruption can cause permanent damage to the vascular system of the penis. We know both statistically and anecdotally that penises are far from permanently-engorged crotch-rocks, and yet almost all sexual discourse on penises is on erect penises, hard penises, penetrating penises.

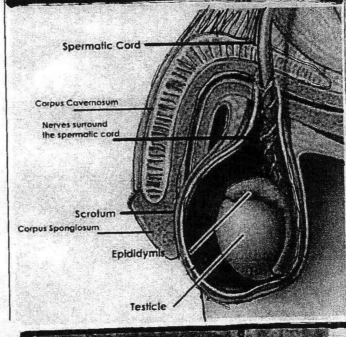

Spermatic Cord
Corpus Cavernosum
Nerves surround the spermatic cord
Scrotum
Corpus Spongiosum
Epididymis
Testicle

+ suck on your date's clit when it's soft

+lube up the glans and fuck her with your hand

+invent new sex practices

+ document everything

+ the frenulum sounds like a carnival ride and you can make it one in your mouth

Why is this significant? Because the operating assumption in our culture is that only hard penises can have sex, that soft penises can't have sex and aren't sexy. This is deeply, deeply incorrect. The major difference between a soft penis and a hard penis isn't whether it can have sex, not whether it can give and receive pleasure, only whether it is hard and can penetrate. That's it. That's the difference. Hardness. And yet there is almost no writing about sex and soft penises except about how to "fix" them by making them hard. It's hard, so to speak, for us to seriously consider the concept of sex with a soft penis because we've been indoctrinated to laugh at the idea. Penises are supposed to be hard, penetrating organs, and definitely not sexy when soft. It's not very fashionable to talk about phallocentrism these days, but I can't think of a better word for the assumption that someone's private parts are useless because they're not hard and, well, phallic.

To put it simply, this is stupid. It's stupid to keep acting like penises are worthless when they are soft, whether that softness lasts a day or six years. We are smarter than that, and it is time to start acting like it. We owe it to the penises in our communities to start playing with them and pleasuring them when they're soft. I think it's a particularly good idea to do this because soft penises are a lot of fun that we're not having, for no good reason.

Contrary to popular belief, a soft penis is not a "Do Not Disturb" sign. Neither is it an accurate indicator of someone's interest, mood, energy level, or libido. Boners are fickle. Sometimes it's not in the cards. Then again, sometimes a boner just happens and the only thing on your mind is how much you don't feel like having one. Your lover-with-a-penis could be counting the seconds until they can get you alone and do filthy, unspeakable things to you and their penis might not so much as twitch. If your lover is a trans woman, there's a rock-solid chance that this happens all the time. There's an equally good chance that it never happens at all. For some of us on testosterone blockers no force in the world could summon an erection. For others there's an impact, and for some there's almost no change whatsoever.

Regardless of how often you have one on your hands, a soft penis doesn't need to be anything other than an opportunity to find out what else it can do besides fill up with blood and poke things.

#4: **Frenulum and Corona**. There are two areas of the glans that are especially sensitive for most penises. The first is the frenulum, the trip of flesh on the underside of the penis that connects the glans to the shaft. The most sensitive part of the frenlum is where it meets the head and forms a sort of Atari symbol, a delta. The delta of the frenulum is very, very sensitive to stimulation. Another part of the glans that is particularly sensitive is the rim, the corona. The least sensate part of a penis is the shaft.

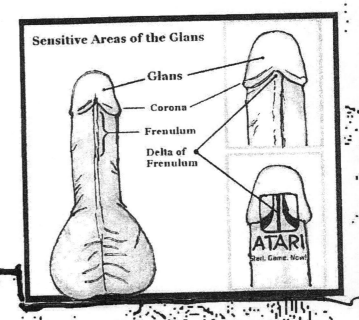

Sensitive Areas of the Glans

Glans
Corona
Frenulum
Delta of Frenulum

ATARI
Start. Game. Now!

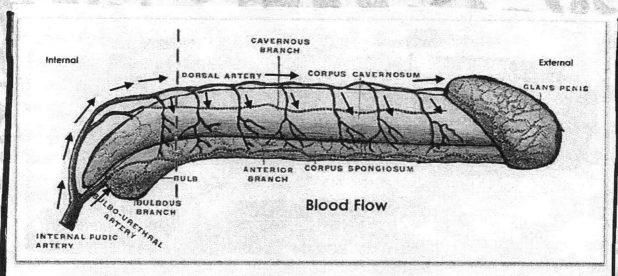

Blood Flow

#5: **Bloodflow.** On the other hand, although the shaft doesn't feel as *much* sensation, it likes a different kind altogether, the kind that comes from pressure. Bloodflow can be a really important part of pleasuring a penis and the place to control it is the shaft. Blood enters and leaves the penis at the base of the shaft on the underside. It fills the spongy and cavernous tissues of the penis to create erections of varying degrees. Erections are maintained by the relatively slow release of blood from the penis back into the veins as they exit. When a penis has trouble staying hard, sometimes this is an effect of leaky blood vessels. The more blood that's in the penis the stiffer it gets and the more taut the skin on the shaft and glans. By increasing pressure to the shaft and squeezing the base of the penis you can keep blood in almost any penis. Once it's in there you'll be able to move it around by squeezing and applying pressure to different parts of the shaft.

Wrap your hand around the base of the penis. Your pinky finger will lie directly across the spot where the dorsal veins and arteries enter the penis.

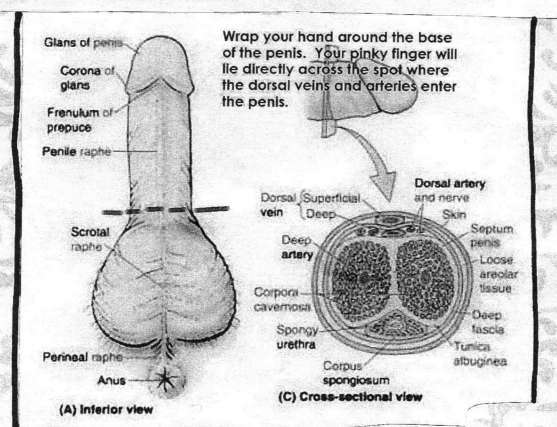

#6: Don't neglect the undercarriage.
You may know the *perineum* by another name, the 'taint,' the fleshy strip of skin between the asshole and the genitals. The sensitive line that you will see running down the middle is the *perineal body,* and beneath that is the prostate (internally.)

The penis, the perineum, the prostate, and the anus share several nerves, and the perineum seems to like those stimulated with pressure. Try rubbing the taint at the same time that you suck or rub the glans. Fun times!

No, but really, don't forget the perineum, it's a popular spot for lots of trans ladies. Get your knee or your thigh in there!

Joke about grinding and dry humping all you want, pressure feels good

nches of the Genitofem

The taint is also a great place to use a vibrator: several major nerve clusters either terminate or pass through the perineum, including the nerve that causes ejaculation. The same nerve branches out to the prostate and the clit/penis.

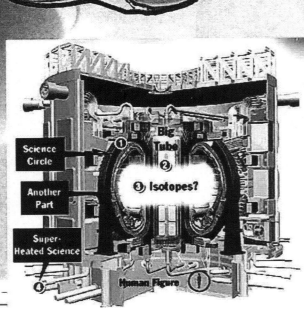

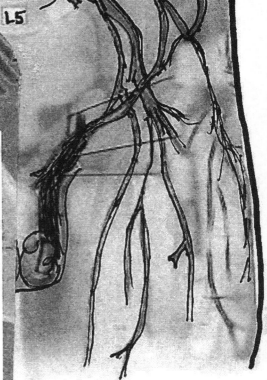

A Science Machine
The expensive device will test and execute more science than ever before

1 Scientists make sure machine's On/Off button is switched to On

2 Parts of the machine begin to move, at first slowly, and then rapidly

3 A lot of science begins to generate

4 Many things light up and sounds of thunder happen

5 Science ends

Science Circle

Another Part

Super-Heated Science

Big Tube
②
③ Isotopes?

Human Figure ①

#7: **Nerves, nerves, nerves.** The penis is an organ designed to experience pleasure and the way it experiences that pleasure is through nerves, which are stretched like a thick web through the penis and crotch. This sounds obvious, but it can be easy to overlook the delicate nature of these nerves and treat the penis like a hunk of meat instead of a delicate instrument. Because, well, the only way we ever see it is from the outside, where it looks like a sausage, not a spider web. Knowing the locations of nerve groups and what they connect to will give you better insight into the various ways that we experience pleasure.

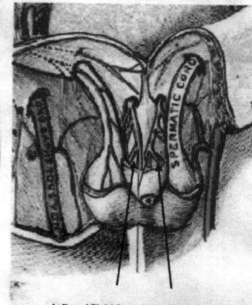

Left and Right Branches of Dorsal Nerve

If the nerves of the penis were celebrities, the most famous would be the pudendal nerve, although it would have to change its name to something with more pizzazz. Let's call it the **P Nerve**. This is the nerve we most often aim to stimulate during sex because it generates the spasms in muscles around the clitoris or penis that produce orgasms and ejaculations. The P Nerve begins in the sacrum at the base of the spine and then forms three branches. One branch goes to the anal sphincter, one to the perineum, and the last branch becomes the Dorsal Nerve of the Phallus. (Medical literature calls it either the dorsal nerve of the penis or dorsal nerve of the clitoris but they have identical functions.) The P nerve is the easiest nerve to stimulate to produce an orgasm. It innervates most of the skin and body of the penis.

P

The P nerve is repsonsible for most orgasms and ejaculation. It runs up either side of the penis along the shaft and then terminates in nerve endings distributed throughout the glans.

Branches of the Genitofemoral Nerve

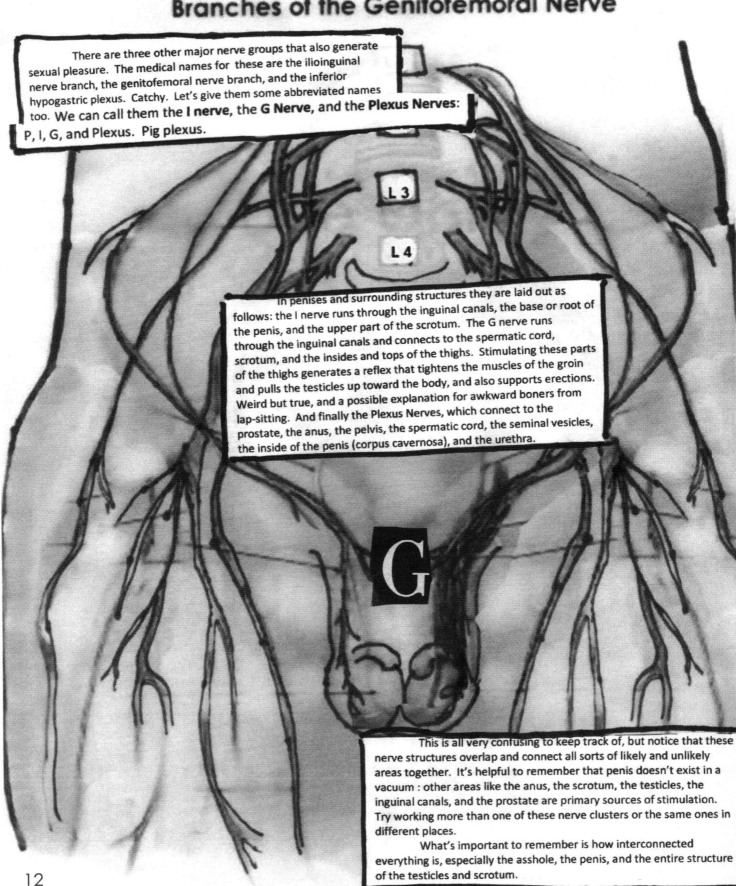

There are three other major nerve groups that also generate sexual pleasure. The medical names for these are the ilioinguinal nerve branch, the genitofemoral nerve branch, and the inferior hypogastric plexus. Catchy. Let's give them some abbreviated names too. We can call them the **I nerve**, the **G Nerve**, and the **Plexus Nerves**: P, I, G, and Plexus. Pig plexus.

L 3

L 4

In penises and surrounding structures they are laid out as follows: the I nerve runs through the inguinal canals, the base or root of the penis, and the upper part of the scrotum. The G nerve runs through the inguinal canals and connects to the spermatic cord, scrotum, and the insides and tops of the thighs. Stimulating these parts of the thighs generates a reflex that tightens the muscles of the groin and pulls the testicles up toward the body, and also supports erections. Weird but true, and a possible explanation for awkward boners from lap-sitting. And finally the Plexus Nerves, which connect to the prostate, the anus, the pelvis, the spermatic cord, the seminal vesicles, the inside of the penis (corpus cavernosa), and the urethra.

G

This is all very confusing to keep track of, but notice that these nerve structures overlap and connect all sorts of likely and unlikely areas together. It's helpful to remember that penis doesn't exist in a vacuum : other areas like the anus, the scrotum, the testicles, the inguinal canals, and the prostate are primary sources of stimulation. Try working more than one of these nerve clusters or the same ones in different places.

What's important to remember is how interconnected everything is, especially the asshole, the penis, and the entire structure of the testicles and scrotum.

Some thoughts on making the most of your P, I, G, and Plexus nerves

Let's strategize some ways to stimulate as many nerves at once as possible.

For Science.

Here's one way to stimulate all four at the same time: fuck your partner in the ass with a dildo in a harness. At the same time, use one of your hands to muff one of her cunts, and the other to rub her clit.

OR let her fuck her own clit while you fuck her reverse cowgirl with both hands in her muff

OR

Anal + Muffing +Oral

OR

Taint + Rimming + Oral

OR

Taint + handjob + Anal

Muffing stimulates the I, G, and Plexus

Anal penetration stimulates the P and Plexus

Anything with the clit stimulates the P nerve; deep clit pressure stimulates the Plexus

Pressure on the perineum stimulates the P nerve and sometimes the plexus

13

Our Mutual Friend

In this issue of the zine I am definitely going to be talking a lot about penises, and I am going to be using the word penis to talk about them. This is a decision, not an assumption or a given, so I want to say a few words about how and why I made it. Basically I needed a word to directly identify the sensitive, fleshy tube of flesh with all the nerves and blood vessels in it. Not everybody uses the same word for this part of their body. I mostly call mine my clit, for instance, but at different times it can be different things. When I am at the doctor's office the word I use is also penis, but not because I believe that's the right word for it. I say penis because when I do both of us understand that I am referencing the aforementioned fleshy tube that is part of my sexy parts. Likewise, I decided that I would use the word penis in this zine, most of the time, to make it clear what I was referring to.

Am I telling you that your body has a penis attached to it? No. Am I making claims about what certain organs *really are*? No, absolutely not. I made the choice to use the word penis because it's the word that most of us will recognize and understand, even if we only need to use it so that we can replace it with a better one *for our own bodies*.

If you don't use that word for your own body and don't like seeing it in this zine, I seriously advise getting out the white-out and replacing it with the words you do like whenever it comes up. Really, I won't mind. The zine won't mind. The zine and I both want you to do what feels good for you.

Our Not-So-Mutual Frien

In this issue of the zine I am also focusing on non-op and pre-op trans women's bodies, because I'm writing from my own experience. This does **not** mean that post-op folks are unwelcome here. You are emphatically, absolutely, without reservation welcome and encouraged to write for this zine. Please. The gap is due to the fact of my own body and my own experiences, and I'm sorry. I wish I knew more, and that is why I need your help. I need you to write about your own body, your own sexuality, your own experiences and knowledge, *because I can't*. Please know that even though we are different, I want you, and other trans women want you. We want to know what you know.

This is true for all kinds of trans women with all kinds of experiences. This zine is not *my* zine, it is *your* zine. It is yours to create and yours to modify and yours to supplement. It will need *all* of our stories and *all* of our knowledge to do what it is supposed to do the best way it can. So please, please, please, understand that if you don't see yourself here, you still *should* and *can* see yourself here. The beauty of this project, and the reason I have chosen to number this issue #0, is that the first voice is not the final voice on any topic. It is an ongoing, open-ended project, really and truly a sexual cookbook for all trans women.

An Illustrated Guide to Muffing and the Inguinal Canals
Basic Technique

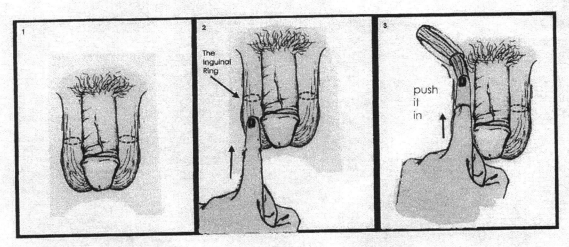

Overview

"Muffing" is the word that I use to describe the act of being fucked in one or both of my inguinal canals. These are twin 'pockets' that are situated in the groin above and behind the testicles and scrotum. They are physically sealed from the outside by the scrotum but can still be penetrated, <u>basically by turning the 'pocket' outside-in.</u> (The technical term for this is "invagination.") The outside-in scrotum then acts as a natural and flexible barrier and either one, or both, can be fucked. There are almost always two inguinal canals, one on each side. In this article I will use the terms "inguinal ring" and "entrance to the inguinal canal" interchangeably. Likewise, I will also use the term "inguinal canal" with the word I use for these parts of my body, my cunts. The inguinal (sounds like linguine) canals are internal passages that hold the testicles inside the body. When the testicles descend during puberty they descend from the inguinals. After puberty the testicles enlarge and the inguinal canals tighten slightly, making it more difficult for the testicles to ascend.

"Tucking" is the word trans ladies most often use to describe the daily practice of binding the genitals. Depending on the woman and her practice, it can be very painful or very comforting or perhaps both. Not all trans women tuck the same way: sometimes all that you need or want to do is push your sexy parts between your legs and pull on your underwear. Sometimes you want most of your "external genitalia" inside of you.

There's also the option of pushing the testicles back up into the body, which sounds a lot more painful than it is. When I mention tucking in this article, this is the kind I'm talking about. This kind of tucking begins with the act of penetrating the inguinal canals with the testicles. Fucking someone by penetrating their inguinal canals is what I refer to as "Muffing" in this article. Whether or not you end up using the *testicles* to penetrate your own cunts, I'm going to show you how to muff by this method first.

Note: I really like getting fucked this way, but it's not for everyone. Many trans women have complicated and/or negative feelings about their biological testicles so please explore and discuss muffing with care.

basically you are shoving the testicles and scrotum back up inside the body

it sounds painful, and at first it is, like so many wonderful things are

but this part of the body was designed to stretch

15

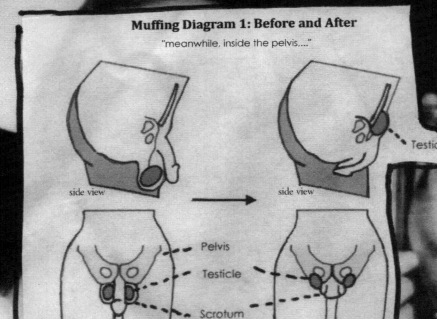

Muffing Diagram 1: Before and After

"meanwhile, inside the pelvis...."

side view → side view

Testicle

Pelvis
Testicle
Scrotum

front view → front view

Untucked   Tucked

This is a cutaway diagram of the pelvis.
It shows where the testicles and things are before and after they are tucked.

Trans women who tuck often learn to push their testicles up into the inguinal canals and to hold them there. Internally the inguinal canals are located on either side of the lower abdomen, just above where the legs join the hips. They are relatively close to the surface, branching upward and outward in the same general direction as the hip bones. Depending on how much and how often the inguinals are being used, they might initially be   difficult to find, but with only a little practice they are actually quite easy to access.

A question I often get is "where's the hole?" The answer is that there is no "hole" or orifice to reach the inguinal canals, because they are covered and enclosed by the scrotum. Instead they are reached by inverting the scrotum and/or testicle that lie below them and pushing them through the inguinal *rings*, found at the base of each testicle. Because they're internal and don't have any external markings indicating their position, it's much easier to find them by touch than by visual reference. This might sound complicated or difficult but it's actually not. The only trick to finding them is to practice and of course to ask for help.

To give you a working image, let's go back to the idea of a pocket turned inside out. Imagine that you turn your pockets out looking for your keys or something. In order to get the lining back into the pocket you don't need a *hole*, you just need to find the edges of the pocket and gently push the lining back inside. The inguinal canal works the same way, but by default the "pocket" is inside out. The edges of the pocket form the inguinal ring.

Muffing Diagram 2: Don't you just love diagrams?

A tucked crotch. The dotted lines show the probable location of the testes. The arrows show the basic direction in which they ascend back into the body: **up and to the sides**.

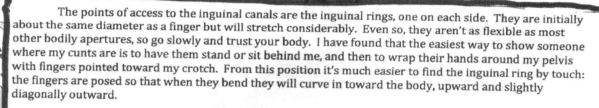

The points of access to the inguinal canals are the inguinal rings, one on each side. They are initially about the same diameter as a finger but will stretch considerably. Even so, they aren't as flexible as most other bodily apertures, so go slowly and trust your body. I have found that the easiest way to show someone where my cunts are is to have them stand or sit behind me, and then to wrap their hands around my pelvis with fingers pointed toward my crotch. From this position it's much easier to find the inguinal ring by touch: the fingers are posed so that when they bend they will curve in toward the body, upward and slightly diagonally outward.

It's good to show a lover how to locate your cunts on their own, but my advice is to expect that they'll need some help for a while: show them your cunts with your own hands. If you're built anything like me, there will be more than enough room for both of you to explore.

It's also good to remind them that your cunts work according to their own rules. Just because they are cunts doesn't mean that they like being fucked exactly like a vagina. The way mine work, for example, the angle of penetration that works best is sort of a diagonal *up and out*. Pushing straight in toward my spine will ram against my pelvic bones and cause pain; pulling the inside wall away from my body hurts just as badly. The techniques that work best on my cunts are the ones that let my cunts be what they are. And with a few delightful exceptions, I'm usually the first one to figure out what makes them feel good and what their limits are.

My conviction is that I'd much rather *show* someone how to fuck me right than depend upon their intuition. I always, always, *always* find my own cunt first, and then help the person who is fucking me to find it itself. This saves a lot of wasted time and needless apologies about not being able to find my body's secret passageways. Personally, I don't really care if someone has trouble finding my cunts; it took me days to learn how to comfortably tuck when I first started, and that was my own body. If my lover hasn't fucked me before, I take a few extra moments to help them, explore, and to show them how my cunts work. It's important to show your lovers what feels good and where all the best spots are.

17

Muffing Diagram 3: The Untucked Gonads and Their Environs

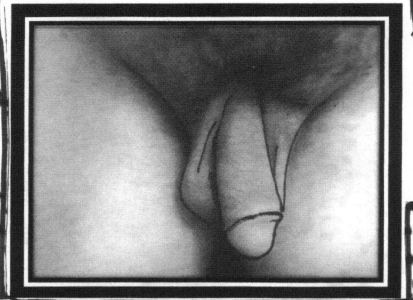

The penis and testicles at rest. The penis normally blocks the testicles so in order to muff, you will need to **lift the penis** (if it doesn't arrange that for you on its own.)

The testicles rest in the scrotum, the sac of incredibly soft skin that corresponds biologically to the labia. Although the scrotum is fused early in development the testicles float in separate tissue compartments joined at the middle, directly beneath the base of the penis. The testicles never actually touch one another, they just share a common wall, like a duplex.

Take a moment to play with the testicles and fondle them. The more you explore the better a feel you'll have for them.

Each testicle is connected to the rest of the body by a spermatic cord wrapped densely in veins, arteries, ligament, and nerve fiber. Gently find these cords and feel along their length. One end will terminate at the testicle, the other will lead directly into the inguinal canal. Be careful with the spermatic cord but don't avoid it entirely; because it's wrapped in nerve fibers it is extremely sensitive. Fondling the spermatic cords may or may not feel good, so keep communication lines open, with your body and with your lover.

Muffing Diagram 4: The Soft Underbelly

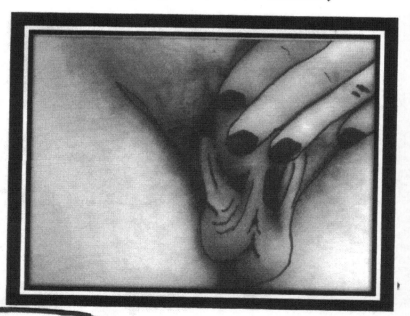

(Ta Dah! The much-maligned testes.)

**Muffing Diagram 5: My Penis' Myspace Picture from 2008
Positioning Your Fingers**

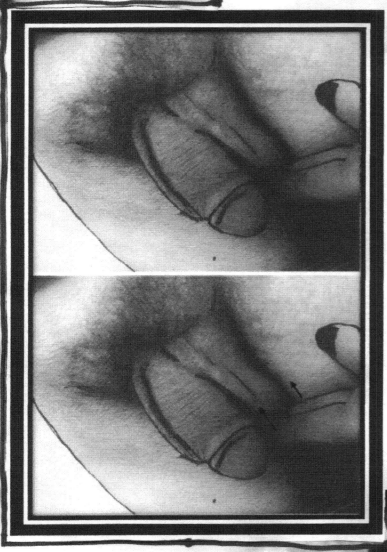

This is the position of the fingers that I've found works best for tucking and muffing. Generally it only takes the first two or three fingers on either hand to gently **lift** the testicle up into the scrotum and through the opening of the inguinal canal. Like any other orifice the inguinal ring generally likes some play and gentle stretching before heavy use.

Initially the inguinal canals won't be able to stretch large enough to accommodate much more than a finger or two, but with time they will stretch and expand. This process can take a long time, so be patient with your body. If you give it time, and work with it rather than against it, you'll be surprised just how much the inguinal canals can be stretched.

But really, avoid the temptation to plunge the depths; instead, spread out slowly. It's better to know your limits than hurt yourself unintentionally.

Note: You might find yourself or someone you have sex with cracking jokes about how 'lez' it feels to use gentle and precise touch rather than fucking a hole for all it's worth. If so, stop what you're doing and make sure that the person you're with isn't an *asshole*: you've just seen a red flag.

You want your lover to treat your cunts well. *You* want to treat your own cunts well. That means being careful and gentle at times, and yes, **they will probably be using their fingers**. Most inguinal canals never stretch wider than an inch or so, and only once, when the testicles descend. If you want to use yours with any regularity you're going to have to love them tenderly, especially at first. Anyone who can't respect that or bring themselves to fuck you with their fingers should not be allowed anywhere near your body.

It's hard to resist a good joke about sage, but the nasty little things that we say about lesbians often come from an equally nasty source: shame and misogyny. When someone uses 'lez' as a pejorative they're shaming women who have sex with women. Let's be clear on that. Even if you're not a woman having sex with a woman this is clearly unacceptable nonsense behavior.

(Cont'd...)

Often what's being shamed are particular kinds of sex, specifically the kinds that focus on nerve stimulation, fine touch and sensation, and efforts to take good care of each other in various ways. **These are actually really good things** and we should be wary of any lover dismissing them more or less because they're uncool. Occasionally I want or need those things, and I won't be shamed for asking for them. I hope that you won't put up with that kind of behavior either.

For your own sake please consider banishing this kind of misogynist garbage from your life. Get out the fucking sage if it helps (told you), but whatever you do don't try to play it cool by fucking the inguinal canals as hard as you can as fast as you can. When it's over you won't just ache, parts of your sex organs will be ruptured. The inguinal canals are flexible, but not as flexible as the other orifices of the body. You can do some real damage if you don't build up gradually and respect the body's limits.

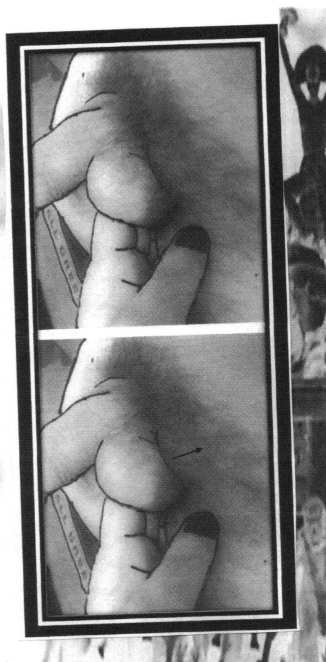

Muffing Diagram 6: Here's the Tricky Part

Before you can push the testicle back into the inguinal canal you have to get it into position. Gently push your first two or three fingers up against the bottom of the scrotum and the testicle in a slightly cupped motion. Keep your fingers gently pressed against the scrotum and the testicle. Stop when the testicle presses against the wall of the abdomen as shown. It will probably look a little bulge-y. Your fingertips should now be pressed very lightly against the bottom of the ovoid testicle, the small point of the 'egg.'

You are basically getting it ready to pop into the inguinal canal.

(A note to our not-trans-woman lovers: It's normal to have trouble doing this at first and getting the positioning right. It's likely that you'll practice this part more than any of the others, and that's the key: practice. Do it as often as you can and sooner or later the feel of it will come to you. Don't feel frustrated. If you get stuck ask your lover to help you out by pushing their testicle up into their cunt for you. Once it's in it's much less difficult to find the opening.)

Muffing might start to sound painful, but again, it's not, or if it is painful, it's painful in a good way, the way anal sex hurts at first

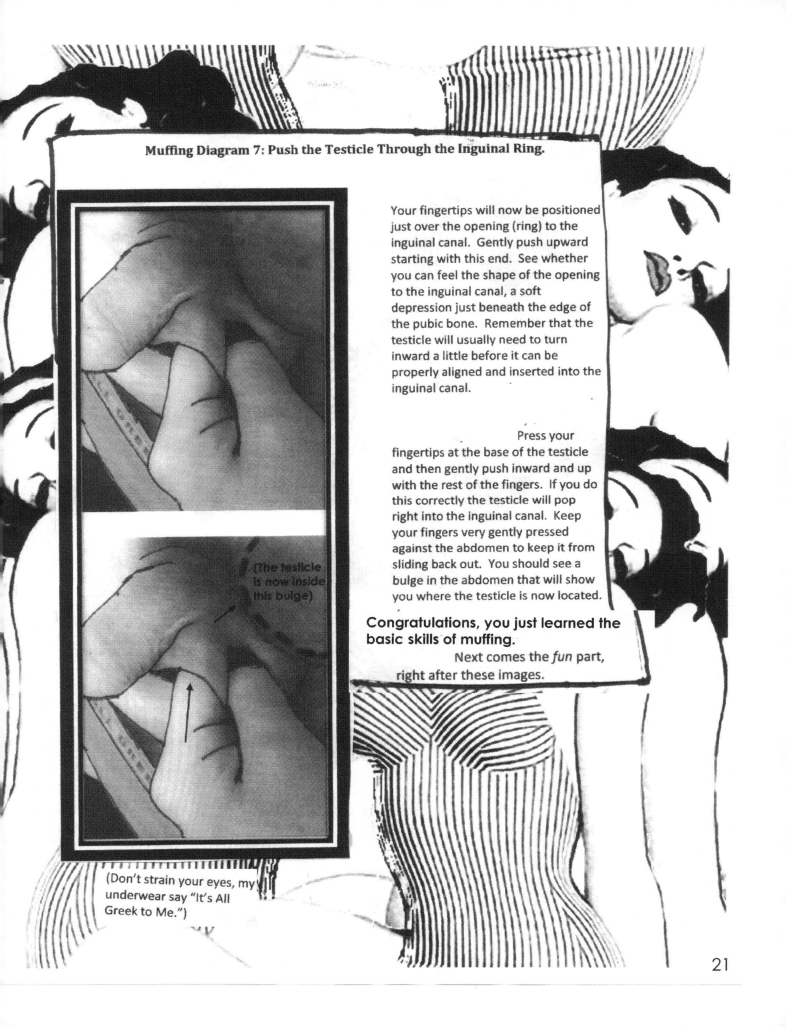

Muffing Diagram 7: Push the Testicle Through the Inguinal Ring.

Your fingertips will now be positioned just over the opening (ring) to the inguinal canal. Gently push upward starting with this end. See whether you can feel the shape of the opening to the inguinal canal, a soft depression just beneath the edge of the pubic bone. Remember that the testicle will usually need to turn inward a little before it can be properly aligned and inserted into the inguinal canal.

Press your fingertips at the base of the testicle and then gently push inward and up with the rest of the fingers. If you do this correctly the testicle will pop right into the inguinal canal. Keep your fingers very gently pressed against the abdomen to keep it from sliding back out. You should see a bulge in the abdomen that will show you where the testicle is now located.

Congratulations, you just learned the basic skills of muffing.

Next comes the *fun* part, right after these images.

(The testicle is now inside this bulge)

(Don't strain your eyes, my underwear say "It's All Greek to Me.")

Muffing Diagram 8

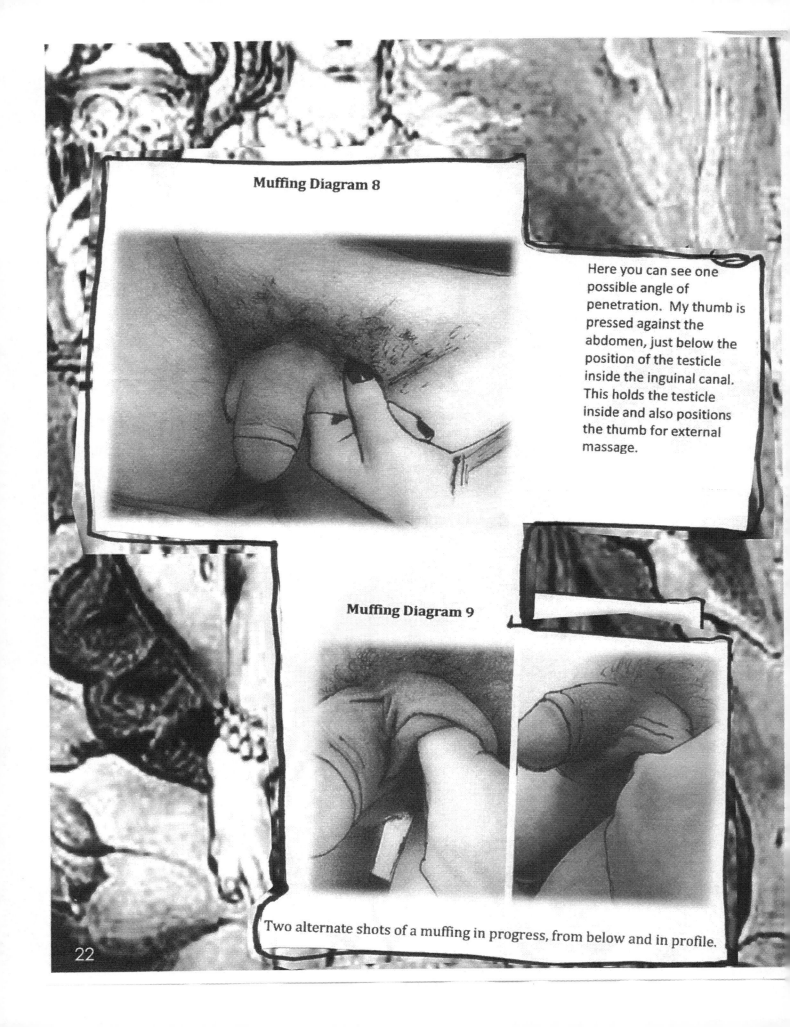

Here you can see one possible angle of penetration. My thumb is pressed against the abdomen, just below the position of the testicle inside the inguinal canal. This holds the testicle inside and also positions the thumb for external massage.

Muffing Diagram 9

Two alternate shots of a muffing in progress, from below and in profile.

Muffing Diagram 10

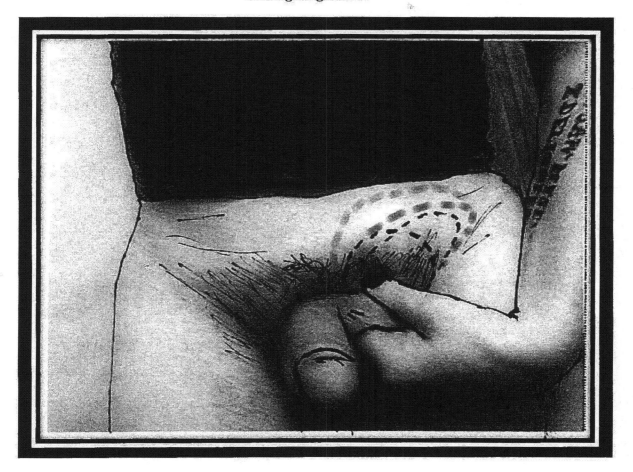

The dotted lines show the approximate boundaries of the <u>inguinal canal</u> when it is penetrated and stretched in various directions. The fainter lines indicate the upper limits of how far I've been able to stretch my own cunts, which may or may not be a helpful guide for your body.

Again, *don't push yourself too far, too fast.* Stretching too far can weaken the walls of the inguinal canal and pull or tear all sorts of sensitive tissue. Don't risk losing your new discovery trying to impress anyone, especially yourself.

What Next?

Once you've gotten yourself into the inguinal canal you can start to explore. You'll find that the shape of the inguinal canals isn't the same as any other kind of hole or bodily orifice. They point outward in the same general direction as the hips and are more or less tube-shaped. They will stretch and expand to some degree with regular activity, but it's *very* important not to push your cunts beyond their limits. I can't stress this enough.

You can use each of the testicles to penetrate its own cunt and follow it in with your fingers, and once you've figured this part out you can also circumvent the balls entirely. You can stick all sorts of things into your cunt! Since there are   two cunts (one canal per testicle) you can also split the difference and fuck each individually and completely differently if you like. The particulars of what feels good and what works best will vary from body to body and person to person. __ let's try walking before running. To get you started, here are a few **very basic ways of** fucking the inguinal canal for beginners:

#1: **Manual Penetration.** Gently push your fingers up through the inguinal ring, and start fucking. Very basic but lots of fun.

#2: **Autopenetration.** (What a sexy word.) Push the testicle in, then let it slide out. Repeat. The testicle stimulates the nerves inside the inguinal canal and in turn the in-and-out movement through the inguinal ring stimulates the testicle. Two distinct nerve centers push against each other as the body literally fucks itself. Also very basic, also lots of fun.

#3: **Massage.** Push the testicle through the inguinal ring and gently hold it in place from the outside. You'll find that the thumb is very useful for this. Now push your fingers into the inguinal canal and massage the testicle, the walls of the cunt, and the nerves of the spermatic cord. Once your fingers are inside, however many feel best, you can also massage from the outside where the testicle bulges against the abdomen. Persistent massage will stimulate spinal nerves and can produce orgasms without even necessarily involving the penis. This takes some patience but it can *really* be worth it.

In issues to come, I hope to hear more about muffing from other trans women. What else have you tried, what works for you, what feels good? What are your favorite things to be penetrated with? And what else do you like to do while you're getting muffed? Do you like someone sucking your clit at the same time, or do you prefer a good rimjob? Keep muffing and start writing!

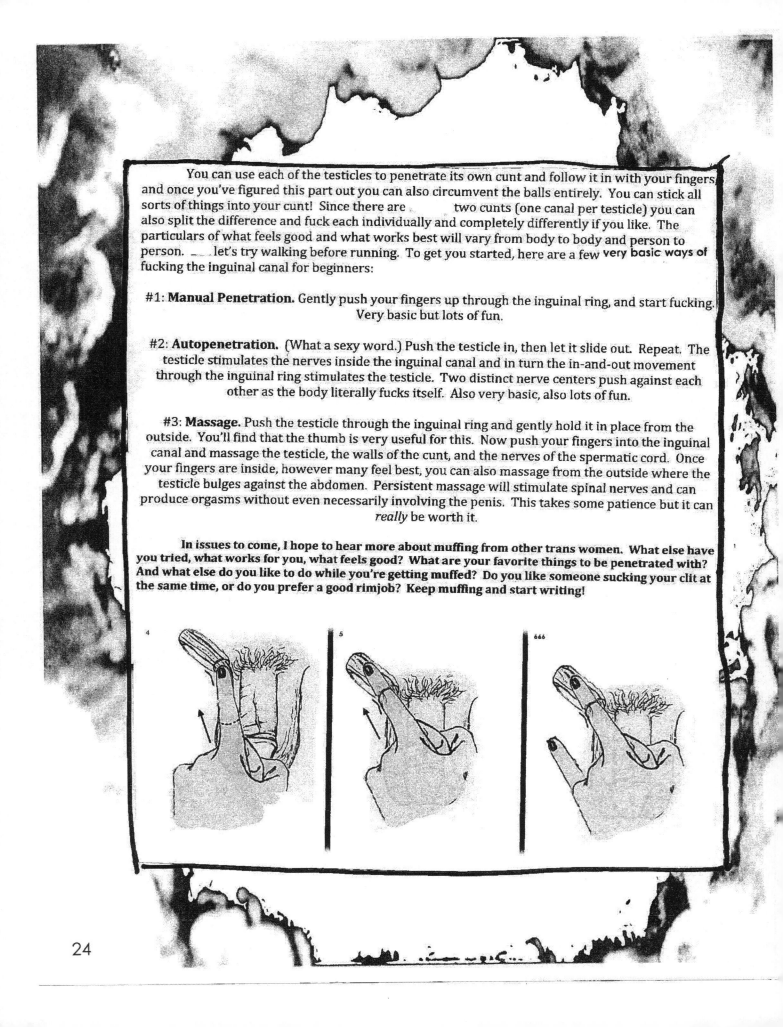

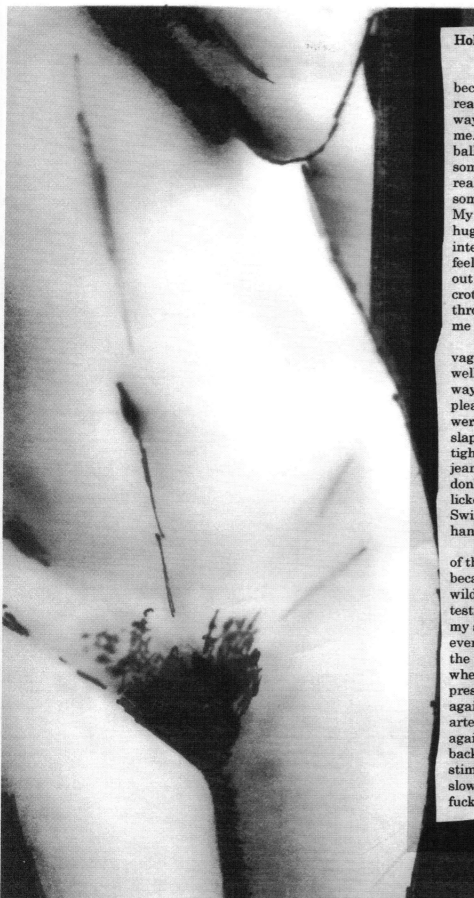

Hold Tight

The reason I started tucking was because I started wearing dresses, but the reason I *kept* it up was because I liked the way it felt to hold part of myself inside me. It's a comforting feeling, having my balls shoved deep up inside. It feels something like how my belly feels after a really big, delicious dinner, and something like getting fucked in the ass. My balls feel cared for, compressed, hugged, squeezed. I feel ripe, deeply interconnected to every part of myself. I feel the spider's web of nerves stretching out through my hips, my bowels, my crotch, all the way up my spine and through the twin, hollow horns inside me: me holding me tight.

For a long time "tucking" felt vaguely uncomfortable, in a good way, well, a painful way, well... it felt lots of ways. I've never gotten any kind of pleasure from my testicles when they were riding outside my body, jauntily slapping against my thighs or pressed up tight against my taint by a tight pair of jeans. I don't like them played with, I don't like them squeezed or really even licked, at least when they're outside. Swinging free, they only feel like lumps hanging from my crotch.

But once they're inside of me, most of these things feel totally different because almost any stimulation drives me wild. When someone plays with my testicles inside me the hair at the base of my spine perks up, I feel tingling through every nerve in my body, right on out to the tips of my fingers and toes. Inside, where the warm is, I like them licked, pressed, fucked, squeezed. They press against the various cords of nerves and arteries of the spermatic cord, they grind against the walls of my abdomen, bounce back and forth against my bladder and stimulate my prostate. My breathing slows, my muscles relax. It hurts so fucking good.

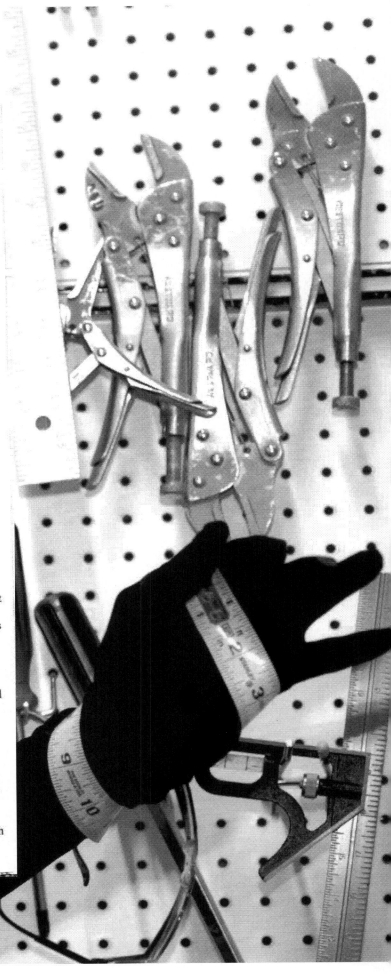

Soft Science

At a certain point when I was a little kid all the little boys started talking (lying) about penis size. I was probably somewhere around 9 or 10 years old and, stereotypically, the little boys would hang out around the jungle gym and talk about sex. There were the usual inaccurate, confused accounts of sex all mixed up in the bullshit lore transmitted by older brothers, cautionary tales from parents, and half-remembered 20/20 specials. One boy insisted that women gave birth out of their asses; another told stories about penises breaking off inside of girls. But the main subject of discussion was always penises and penis size.

It seems reasonable to me most little boys get preoccupied with penises at a certain point, usually well before they actually start causing any trouble. I mean, they're kind of a big deal for boys, (although potentially not *as* big a deal as they are to the girls who have them,) and they look weird. Also, at that age it's hard to know how to feel when you realize that, someday, someone will want you to put the thing that you pee out of inside their body. For fun.

But looking back, what seems really strange to me isn't that the little boys at my school were talking about the size of their dicks. In fact, they shied away from that topic, probably because they feared along with everyone else that they were much, much smaller than they should be. But they still *loved* talking about big dick; they just preferred talking about their *dad's* big dick and their *brothers'* big dicks. I have no way of knowing whether that's typical, but I hope so. It's vaguely reassuring to imagine that all of the shitty little boys who used to bully me were constantly daydreaming about monstrously large cock.

Anyway, because these little size queens talked about their dad's big cocks during recess every day, I soon had the impression that penises were typically well over twelve inches long and five inches thick. And once I had a number in my head, it was only a matter of time before I did the inevitable scientific comparison. So one Fall night after everyone else had gone to bed, in a corner of my dad's office, I nervously held my hairless, soft little penis against the cold yellow metal of a tape measure. I looked at the black lines and numbers with horror and thought to myself, "Oh my god, I'm tiny! Four inches has to be the smallest penis in *history*!"

It seemed obvious to my 10 year old brain that penises are soft most of the time, so that was how I measured mine each of the four or five times I re-checked it in my early teens.   I finally learned *slightly* more realistic penile dimensions as well as the embarrassing fact that they were usually measured hard. Both facts were obtained from the usual source of hard scientific teenage data on sex: old men at a barber shop.

Soft Bodies
Erotically Flaccid

As far as I can tell, soft penises are one of the most neglected subjects in studies of sexuality. That's not to say that no one is talking about soft penises, because plenty of people are, but they're only talking about how to make them hard. I've yet to find a single article, essay, story, or description of a sexy soft penis. The very idea that a soft penis could be sexy is a little hard for most people to grasp, so to speak, and the suggestion that it could be just as much fun as a hard one is even, well, harder. Search Google or most books on sex for mentions of un-erect penises and the most you are likely to find is suggestions for how to make them hard. If you're lucky you might find a mention that you don't need a hard penis to have sex, which is completely accurate, but also entirely ignores the question of how to pleasure a soft penis or get pleasure from one.

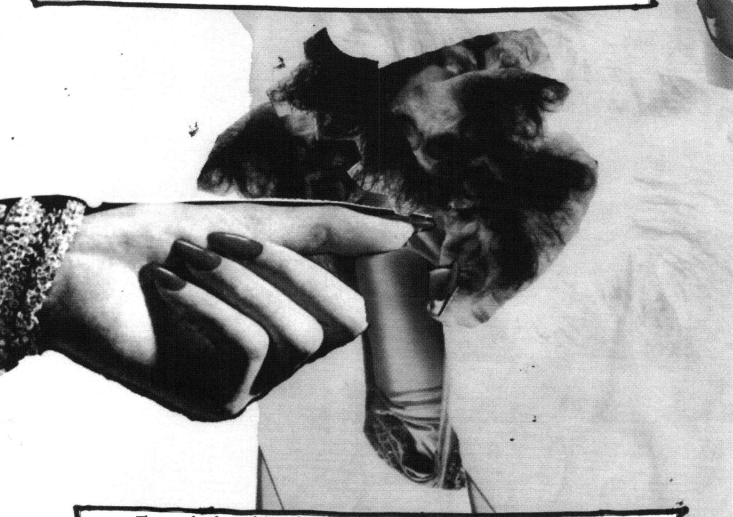

The annals of sex advice columns and sexual horror stories are full of soft penises, as well as descriptions of the response that men and women and everyone else typically have to them: a combination of disappointment, pity, and horror. They're the punch line of a joke with no setup, no content, only mute assumptions and expectations that all cocks are rock-hard. If not, they're assumed to be useless or pathetic or both.

To illustrate how massively unimaginative this assumption is, consider the completely obvious fact that just about half of the population functions sexually without ever having had a penis, a fact that is nonetheless worth repeating as often as it needs saying.

Sexual expectations of penises and cocks begin with the assumption that they are stiff, firm, hard as wood. But by the numbers, penises spend most of their time being soft and yielding. Some statistics might helpfully illustrate this. These statistics are mostly about *men*, but bear with me, sexology has simply not caught up with trans people.

For instance, penile erections typically last somewhere around 30-40 minutes. The average number of erections a penis has per day varies considerably between individuals but after a quick scan of statistics on masturbation, sex, and spontaneous erections, 3 per day would probably be a generous average for anyone over the age of 22. So let's say that on an average day, most penises are erect for about an hour, perhaps two. That means that penises are erect less than 10% of the time, and that is a pretty generous figure. Ten percent is also the approximate figure given for the number of people with penises who will have "erectile dysfunction" or "impotence" at some time in their life.

Now, I have no doubt that for lots of men in our culture not being able to have an erection when you want one is really very stressful, and I don't discount the shame or suffering it must represent. However, I'm wary of categorizing anything that affects 10% of a population as a disorder. I'm also skeptical of the 10% statistic, because it's been estimated from the number of men who self-report recurring difficulty having an erection. It's likely that the number is so low because *more men aren't self-reporting*, and because many men don't consider occasional difficulty to be erectile dysfunction.

I passionately despise the term "erectile dysfunction" almost as much as I dislike the word impotence because both terms are used to shame and pathologize soft penises and name them as asexual, ineffective, un-erotic, and troublesome. Let me suggest that in addition to the many and varied treatments currently available for "ED," we should also consider the not-so-radical possibility that we're going about this the wrong way. Because penises can be just as sexy when they're not erect.

Over the past several months I've spent hours looking for something written on the topic of pleasuring soft penises, and you might not be shocked to discover that I found nothing. In short, when sex advice columnists, doctors, sex educators, or anyone else talks about non-erect penises, they're probably talking about ways to make them erect. Occasionally someone mentions that, just because you're having sex with a person who has a penis, that doesn't mean that penis has to be hard and penetrating. But so far as I can gather no one has actually proceeded to write suggestions for what to *do* with a soft penis. There's no guide, no ideas, no suggestions beyond "make it hard" or "do something else." What a lamentable state to find ourselves in, that after decades of progressive and sex-positive sex education and practice soft penises are still treated like a fifth wheel.

So here are a few ideas for how to use and play with a soft penis, including some ideas for how to make it easier to talk about and explore your lover's body.

First of all, it's important to create a good space for playing with a soft penis. This can mean lots of things, so perhaps the best thing you can do is introduce the topic in conversation and listen to what your lover says. "Let's talk about when this is soft." Likely the best time and place for such a conversation is *not* after your date has had or attempted to have an erection. For instance. I am of the opinion that playing with a soft penis shouldn't be treated like a sort of runner-up activity to the various things you can do with an erect one. So my advice is to set aside time and space for playing with each other's bodies.

28

If you're both into it, taking a bath together can be a good way to keep things relaxed as well as comfortably intimate. I like that bathtubs put you in very close quarters. They make you touch each other a lot and press against each other, and they're not particularly dignified, which cuts down on pretension and pride. For my money they're one of the best places to get to know someone else's body *as* a body. But whether you find that space in a bed, on a couch, in a bath tub, or sitting in the middle of the floor, the bottom line should be making each other comfortable. If you can create safe space for playful and interested exploration of the genital terrain, you're likely to come up with new ideas as well as useful questions, and also have a good time.

Second, wherever you station yourselves, go out of your way to *play*. Ask the person you're fucking to play with themselves, and emphasize that you're not necessarily talking about masturbation, but literally *playing* with their penis. Play around with your body and keep conversation moving, and ask to play with their body as well. With permission, get your fingers and hands right in there and start exploring, touching, rubbing, and stretching. Ask the person you're fucking (what a sexy phrase) to let you know how things are feeling and talk as much about their body as they want. Ask them to talk about what feels good and why, and about what doesn't feel good and why.

Soft penises like to be touched in very different ways than hard ones. In my experience you're more likely to be stimulating nerve endings and nerves much deeper in the tissue that might respond to completely different kinds of sensation than when erect. Trust that your lover will let you know if you're doing something uncomfortable. With trans women in particular, you're likely to find more emotional discomfort than physical, but if you do pinch something or cause some pain, wait a moment and then ask to continue. Don't panic. Penises are remarkably flexible and pliable, *especially* when they're not erect. The skin and tissue of a penis can stretch all sorts of ways, and there are major nerves and nerve ending running all through the penis and its surrounding neighborhood. Penises can work very differently soft, and you'll find tremendous variation between them. Whether you have a penis yourself or not, you're likely to learn a few things about penises, and in particular about the penis that is right in front of you.

This is all well and good, and very important stuff, but you may be asking what kinds of **sex acts** you can actually *do* with a soft penis. The answer will vary from person to person, but for me the answer is "almost anything." Practice safer sex by using condoms and other barriers if there's going to be contact with any fluids **or** mucous membranes. Remember that our friend the penis doesn't need to be erect to ejaculate. Soft penises usually aren't too much trouble to get into a condom after you practice a little. So get a condom on it and start finding out what feels good.

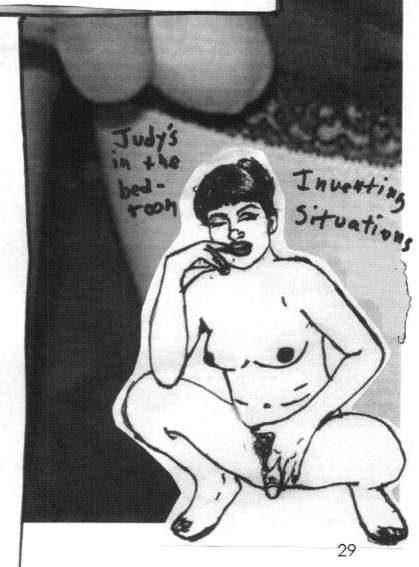

Judy's in the bed-room

Inventing Situations

29

You can fondle and pet a soft penis just as well as a hard one, maybe even better. You can fuck a soft penis with your hands, your mouth, or pretty much any other part of your body. You can rub a soft penis any way conceivable. You can go down on a soft penis. The glans is incredibly sensitive whether hard or soft, so my suggestion is to start there. The underside of the penis can be another hot spot, as well as the base. But also find the major nerves and other sensitive spots and try out different kinds of touch on them. Some penises want to feel lots of pressure, while others might prefer surface sensation and touch.

Keep in mind that a soft penis is extremely flexible and use that to your advantage. You can stimulate skin and tissue and keep them rolling and sliding and moving around with a lot less effort than it takes to work the shaft of an erect penis. If you're used to penises showing pleasure by getting hard (and depending on the penis you're pleasuring, it might do just that at some point,) you might feel a little unsure of how to tell that what you're doing feels good. This is exactly why it's so important to keep your lover talking, and talking about what their body is feeling.

Check in from time to time and explicitly ask your partner to vocalize what feels good and why, and also to talk about what they might like. For trans women in particular it *can* be very important and productive to treat a soft (or hard) penis as you would a cis woman's clit. This is especially important when a woman thinks of, experiences, and uses her body in those terms. Again, keep the lines of communication open and active, and be prepared to see a lot of variation, between sexual partners and between encounters.

you can actually do more with a soft penis than a hard one

IF

you are creative

Some trans women like fucking and penetrating with their own genitals, and likewise lots of us like getting blowjobs, especially if they're done enthusiastically and well. But keep in mind that a soft penis works differently, so going down might look and feel very different. Personally I don't find that blowjob skills translate very effectively to a *soft* penis. But on the other hand, knowing how to fuck a girl with your mouth seems to translate very well to a soft penis. Remember to lubricate. But most importantly, remember your own enthusiasm and pleasure. If you're not having fun after a while, *find* a way to have fun or move on to something else. Fucking is all about having a good time with someone else. Otherwise, what's the point?

Our bodies are not hard by nature. The bones and nails and cartilage gristle in us are our hardest pieces, but they can also be the most fragile, the most brittle. Under the surface of our pliable skin are veins, soft subcutaneous fat, rubbery nerves, joints, meaty muscles, and squishy organs . We have asses, we have tits, we have bellies. We have second chins, we have muffin tops, we have thighs. Where there isn't fat, there's water, in our blood and muscles. All in all our bodies are somewhere between 50-70% water. Our bodies are so very soft.

In so-called mainstream culture hard bodies have been popular for a very long time, especially for men. It's no secret that our actors and models tend to be grotesquely thin; they're lean, bone-dry, apparently cut from wood, like Edward Norton in "Fight Club." They're so… solid that in movies they can survive being hit by cars or punch their way out of buried coffins with only a little blood to show for it. We live in a culture that venerates hard bodies above all other types, especially when it comes to masculine bodies.

Our "heroes" these days don't qualify by having brilliant minds, excellent morals, superior compassion, or making great things. Instead their main qualification is that they can crawl through broken glass and gunfire and emerge, perhaps bloody, tired, likely coated in a thick layer of soot for no evident reason, **but still _hard_.** John McClintock, Jack Bauer, and every male cast member of "LOST" except Hurley, yes I *am* looking at you. **Put your shoes on.**

As much as I love them, our comic book superheroes are the worst of the lot: even in the 21st century their bodies are _still_ fashioned from clay or made of steel or rock. They clothe themselves in iron, wear metal gauntlets, carry big stone hammers, and sport claws or shields made from unbreakable metal. They wear armor over leather over muscles so taut you can see the outlines of their internal organs.

I don't think that anyone has ever complimented me on how sexy my penis looks when it's soft, but whatever, it's totally sexy.

But is hardness really all that?
One of my favorite essays on sexuality, desire, and pornography is Angela Carter's The Sadeian Woman, a distinctly sex-positive and bdsm-positive book published in 1979, at a time when that kind of thinking was still unfashionable. In her "polemical preface" Carter lays down some of the smartest shit I've ever read about the ideology of pornography and normative sexuality. Pornography, she says,

…involves an abstraction of human intercourse in which the self is reduced to its formal elements. In its most basic form, these elements are represented by the probe and the fringed hole, the twin signs of male and female in graffiti, the biological symbols scrawled on the subway poster and the urinal wall, the simplest expression of stark and ineradicable sexual differentiation, a universal pictorial language of lust – or, rather, a language we _accept_ as universal because, since it has always been so, we conclude that it must always remain so.

31

Basically, the formal elements of human sexuality as we usually represent them are a hole and something that goes into the hole, a cock or a dildo or a fist. This has huge implications for what we think of sex that doesn't fit this description, and as sex-positive and open minded as all of us are, the ideology of our culture still bears down on us and makes it difficult to appreciate sexuality that doesn't fit this shape. Carter, writing in 1979 and partly in response to anti-pornography feminists and lesbian feminist theory, is mostly concerned with appraising what value there is in pornography as an art and as a practice that, she believes, can be salvaged.

"Pornographers are the enemies of women," she writes, "**only** because our contemporary ideology of pornography does not encompass the possibility of change, as if we were the slaves of history and not its makers, as if sexual relations were not necessarily an expression of social relations, as if sex itself were an external fact, one as immutable as the weather, creating human practice but never a part of it." But of course that's exactly what sex is: a human practice. And we can change it in all sorts of ways, usually little by little but sometimes in big ways. Each of us has an ongoing relationship to sexuality that is something like a negotiation. We can't *escape* sex or pornography any more than we can escape any other kind of ideology. And who would want to?

But we can reshape the way we talk about and understand our bodies. That's actually pretty amazing. The elasticity we enjoy in our words and minds is extensive. Our bodies are bound by the ideas and words we have at our disposal, but we're like a figure in a painting that has her own, real pencil to draw on top of what is already there. Like a pencil the changes we make can also be changed by others. But at least we've got a pencil.

Trans women's bodies are soft bodies, firstly because our bodies are human bodies. Our bodies can also be soft because they *feel* soft, or *because we say they are*. So much of what we are and how we feel is about how we frame it. Softness is like that.

So our bodies can be soft bodies. And I am going to go a step further and say that they *should* be soft bodies. I'm not talking about the message that all women are given that our skin should always be made buttery-soft, usually by using X product. I am saying that we should make a commitment to noticing the parts of us that are soft and respecting them. We should make a practice of enjoying both the hard and soft parts, and the fact that they frequently alternate. Muscles work in groups and some are always at rest, unflexed, soft. Our flesh is soft. It is beautiful soft. It is sexy soft. It is *soft enough already* and never *not hard enough*.

Soft is pretty. Soft is sexy. Soft is beautiful.

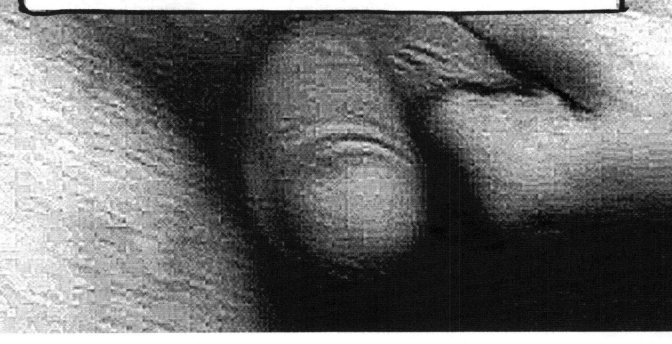

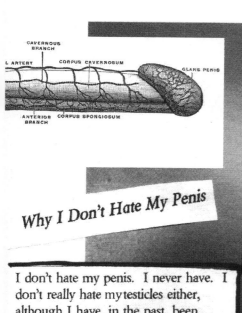

Why I Don't Hate My Penis

I don't hate my penis. I never have. I don't really hate my testicles either, although I have, in the past, been puzzled by them at times. But hate? Never. I'm not sure why this is, but I feel lucky. Most of the trans women I know feel ambivalent about their sexy parts at best, and lots of us do hate the parts we were born with. So why am I different?

It's tempting to say that liking my body is a sign of being well-adjusted, but I know that's not true. For lots of us a change is exactly what we need, for trans folks in particular. There are other parts of my body that I feel dysphoric about, and I think more than anything it's a happy accident that my penis escaped that fate. On the other hand, it might actually feel easier to be a trans woman (and perhaps I would have transitioned sooner) if I had always felt disconnected from my penis. It makes explaining my situation slightly more difficult when I have to add that, in addition to being a transsexual, I am not actually interested in changing my genitals at all.

And it makes my life more difficult that what I have between my legs is not just a penis, it's a woman's penis. That's something that took me a little while to put into words, but those are the right words. *My body is a woman's body and part of it is my penis*, a woman's penis. (You can also call it a lady penis if you want to, I think it's lady-identified.) But what does that mean in practice?

It means that my penis wants different things than most penises, and as I've gotten better at listening to it my sexual practices have changed somewhat. I knew early on that while I was into fucking someone with a cock, my penis was only into occasional cock-being. The rest of the time it would rather be a clit, and for the most part that's how I treat her. She likes to be sucked, rubbed, all of the usual things. Really the only difference is size, the hole at the tip, and every so often she wants to get into penis-drag and fuck someone's mouth, cunt, or asshole. In that way we're well-matched: I also enjoy occasional boy-drag. I think for both my penis and myself, the part that feels gross is the coercive assumption that because we look like we do, we should want to behave masculinely all of the time.

33

"My body is a woman's body and part of it is my penis"

As I said, I figured out early on that my penis was only occasionally interested in penetration. This is usually one of the first things I tell new lovers when we have our 101 (or at least 1-on-1) talk: yes, that's an option, but only every so often and *only* when I'm in the mood. Failure to hear me on that can have some pretty significant negative consequences; I clam up, I cross my arms. Being asked to fuck someone with my penis as a cock generally puts me off, and sometimes enough that I get angry or upset. I don't understand the desire. Or I do, but I'm defiant: why ask for the smaller, unreliable, and most importantly *uncooperative* cock when there are plenty of dildos available? When I try to force the issue on my penis she is even more defiant: she basically crosses her arms as well, and things get difficult and annoying.

For a few years I misinterpreted this as a problem with my libido, but then I started paying better attention to my body: my libido was just fine, I masturbated all the time. I was almost always interested in fucking but usually my penis didn't feel like penetrating anything. This is a difficult sensation to describe but it's one that I am utterly familiar with: the dull ache of wanting to get fucked emanating from my clit.

To explain very inelegantly, it feels just like when I want to get fucked in the ass, but inside out, and on the other side.

Until I discovered my cunts (the inguinal canals) this was frustrating because there was nothing to *get* fucked. At this point I know myself well enough to understand how I can satisfy that urge, and that it doesn't come from lack of libido but from having a woman's penis. The key to figuring that out was thinking of my body differently. As a woman's body, yes, but also as parts that communicated and negotiated with my brain.

I think that's a very trans way to think about one's body: that it can have its own opinions about what it is and what it wants, quite apart from the brain. The nerves that generate sexual feeling are, after all, spinal nerves that more or less only communicate with the brain by *sending* information, not receiving commands. But of course not only trans people can and do understand their bodies this way. The people I hear talking about their bodies this way are disabled folks, older people, sometimes fat-identified people; what I hear that sounds familiar to me isn't so much the content of their words but the agency they give to their bodies. I think this is because our bodies don't always function in the same way as others, for whom the world is designed, and so we begin to pay attention to our bodies' messages.

the squeaky wheel gets the grease, or in this case the attention necessary to really *hear* what it's saying.

I would never tell another trans woman how to feel about her genitalia, but I think I do want to invite anyone reading this, trans woman or otherwise, to try listening to the body more closely. It may be the case that your parts are telling you that they need to change in order to give you pleasure, or it may be the case that they are telling you things that you haven't paid close enough attention to hear. I hope that whatever is going on, you find your own strategies for working *with* your body rather than against it whenever it's possible. After all, it's rude to ignore a lady.

TALKING
SEX

"Second Guessing Your Orgasms"

When I describe sexual experiences I often second-guess my own body, interrogate my own memories and sensations and doubt the legitimacy of my experiences.
"Nobody else has ever told me that they've felt that before – am I just imagining things?"
"Is what I'm trying to describe even possible?"

I try to remind myself that these unproductive doubts and fears can only occur to me because most of the time I have no frame of reference for my body except my own body.

Strap-ons and Toys

Getting my first harness was unequivocally one of the most important moments in my sexual development. I had used toys for years, I love toys, but for some reason I just couldn't get it through my head that it would be a good idea to get a harness. I thought I would hurt myself squeezing my penis against the inside of the harness and that I would look silly. Maybe I look silly in a harness, maybe I look silly all the time. Who knows? But trans women look hot in a harness. Almost nothing gets me hotter.

And let's talk about practical: whether you have frequent and firm erections or never have them at all, a dildo will beat you in 9 out of 10 tests, certainly for endurance. Dildos are safer than fucking someone with a part of your own body, they're washable, they are interchangeable and come in a wider variety of shapes and colors.

Dildos let me fuck someone with a cock without using a part of my own body *as* a cock. Harnesses don't just help me fuck other people with a cock that isn't mine, that isn't a part of my body. They also accentuate the distinction between my sexy parts and "my cock." I love how my clit feels poking out of the top of my harness or dangling out the side I feel hypersexual and also thoroughly and distinctly a woman when I wear a harness. Harnesses help me feel my dyke-ness, my woman-ness. When I wear a harness and tuck, the harness holds my g-spots inside my cunts and also pushes against them and protects them.

My only regret about harnesses is that I haven't yet found one with two O-rings as well as a good design for the straps that accommodates my whole sexy package, leaving the perineum and asshole free. I really like anal sex whether I'm giving or receiving, so sometimes it's important that I have access to everything. Usually I have to compromise, which truthfully isn't the end of the world.

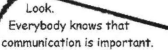

communication

Look.

Everybody knows that communication is important. We know deep down that the more you talk about sex the better it will be. That's how it works.

But I want to debunk a persistent myth that kept popping up during my calls for submissions to the zine and during the survey that I put out, the myth that **the sole secret of good sex is communicating** with the person you're having sex with. **You need more than good communication skills to have good sex, you need to have good sex skills.**

I was told more than once that this zine did not need to exist because the secret to good sex, as everyone knows, is just good communication.

BULLSHIT.

Good communication depends on knowing what you want to do and how to do it. I'm not saying that you don't know these things, I'm saying that all the communication in the world will do you not a bit of good unless you know, A, how to fuck, and B, how you like to get fucked.

These are in fact not skills that we are magically gifted with: sex is a skill and it is learned like any other skill. There are as many ways to fuck as there are combinations of people in this world, and ideas in their heads, and none of those ways of fucking come to any of us naturally.

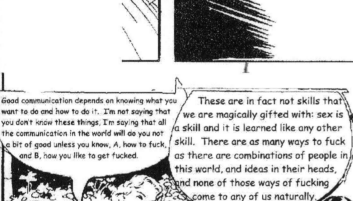

We learn how to suck cock, eat pussy, give a rimjob, use a dildo, fist someone, rub one out, give a handy, or have PIV intercourse.

These are all skill sets that we learn and it is time to give them their due. They are skills that you have, if you already have them, and if you do not then you do not know how to do that thing until you learn HOW.

When you do not have the language for what you want, communication will not help you say what you want.

39

SAFETY TIPS FROM ANUBIS

DID YOU GET ANY OF THAT?

NOT A FUCKING WORD.

in order to communicate effective you have to speak the same language *and* know what you're doing, otherwise it's all hieroglyphics.

imagine learning how to drive a car entirely through verbal instructions with no actual time spent behind the wheel, and then getting into a corvette all by yourself

Can you communicate your way to a better blowjob? Yes, you can. But wouldn't you rather that the person giving you a blowjob has lots of experience, and knows lots of tricks to make you curl your toes?

Well, that is,...

In other words, wouldn't you ra get a blowjob from someone wh knows how to give a blowjob?

Communicating: Some Suggestions

First of all, does the person you're having sex with have the same vocabulary that you do? Often the answer will be "no" for one reason or another. They might be a straight cis guy who has no idea about anything, or they might be an eager and educated queer, or even another trans woman, and *still* have no idea what the words that you are using mean to you. You have to share your vocabulary with your lovers so that they know what you're talking about.

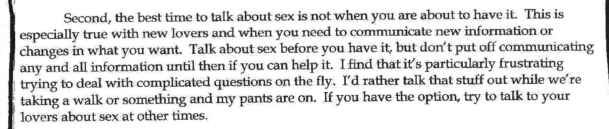

Second, the best time to talk about sex is not when you are about to have it. This is especially true with new lovers and when you need to communicate new information or changes in what you want. Talk about sex before you have it, but don't put off communicating any and all information until then if you can help it. I find that it's particularly frustrating trying to deal with complicated questions on the fly. I'd rather talk that stuff out while we're taking a walk or something and my pants are on. If you have the option, try to talk to your lovers about sex at other times.

Third, remember that being trans doesn't mean you're the only one who needs to communicate things. Communication is not a monologue, it is a conversation with input from both sides. You are indeed a special and unique gender snowflake, and so is your partner whatever their identity or identities.

Fourth, there *are* some specific things that trans ladies usually want to talk about. Some of these include **what's up with our sexy parts** (what to call them, how they can be used or not used,) **what's up with our language**, (what we like to be called, what we don't like to be called,) **how we want to fuck,** (what kinds of sex acts we're into or not into,) and where our **"no-zones"** are if we have any. Other folks like to be asked these things too.

Other communication tips:

+ Think before you speak. **But do speak up.**
+ Give compliments. Try to make them about things your lover likes about herself.
+ Don't ask medical questions, period. It's not your business. If she decides to share, she will.
+ Learning about me is your responsibility, not mine. This is another version of the ever-so-popular "I am not here to educate you." It's true. Do some work on your own please.

41

And Now, A Pubic Service Announcement
"Jizz, The Great White Whale"

(Note to the reader: I invite you to read this article as if it were spoken aloud by Scott Baio, TV's Charles in Charge and the narrator of several sexual education films screened in my junior high school. In the finer classrooms of my 6th, 7th, and 8th grade Health Science classes I had the distinct pleasure of watching Chachi from Happy Days discussing pubic hair, body odor, menstruation, and penises. Therefore, in my mind, Scott Baio's voice is permanently linked to any and all discussions of semen. It is my hope that I can share this happy association with you as you read.)

Before I begin this article about sperm, I should probably admit: I really, *really* hate talking about sperm. This is one of the first articles I wanted to write for the #0 issue specifically because I'm so sick of talking about it. Of all the many particularities and differences about having sex with trans women, this is probably the only subject that I am ready to *stop* talking about. Preferably forever. Unfortunately, so long as my body continues to make sperm and I continue to be a big homo, that's an unrealistic desire. But even though I don't have the luxury of pretending sperm doesn't exist, I am certainly ready for others to start picking up the slack on this topic. Frankly I am eager for more people I know to start educating themselves about sperm and pregnancy so that they know how to act right when the topic comes up.

The reason I hate talking about sperm is that my body makes it. Because my body is a woman's body and because most of my sexual partners are queer women, this routinely presents me with some really irritating and shameful problems, in fact several million of them for each drop of semen I produce.

I hate reaching those moments when a lover realizes that my cum is also jizz, that it could get them pregnant, and they begin treating my cum like radioactive waste.

Not everyone does this, and it's not like I don't understand when they do. I want to get someone pregnant just *slightly* less than I want 100 years of diarrhea. I have experienced a thoroughly average number of pregnancy scares and pregnancy realities. It's difficult to express why those experiences felt particularly awful to me as a trans woman, but I'm going to give it my best effort.

If I have unprotected sex with a cis woman or a trans man, there is always a chance that no matter how many hormones I've drowned my balls in, I could get someone pregnant. That scared me before I transitioned for all the normal reasons, and because I knew that I was going to eventually transition. Post-transition, pregnancy is scary. When I have to consider the possibility of pregnancy happening to my lover, I'm reminded forcefully and unwillingly of my sex life as a boy. To state the obvious *talking about my sperm makes me feel like a boy again in a really bad, bad way.* Having a conversation about the possibility of pregnancy can often be difficult, too, because depending on my lover's experience and how much they have done their homework, these are often the moments when I am asked the most emotionally difficult, inappropriate, or bizarre questions about my body.

Typically I am asked questions about my body that I have no answers for, like what my sperm count is and how statistically likely it is that I will knock someone up.
Nobody knows this stuff, and no one should have to.
Make contingency plans, but don't worry about statistical likelihoods.

I practice safer sex, but although my sexual partners are almost always impeccably knowledgeable about STIs, fluid exchange, and safer sex practices, the sad reality is that for most of them my sperm represents the first time they have had to seriously consider the possibility that they could get knocked up.

42

† never tell me the odds!

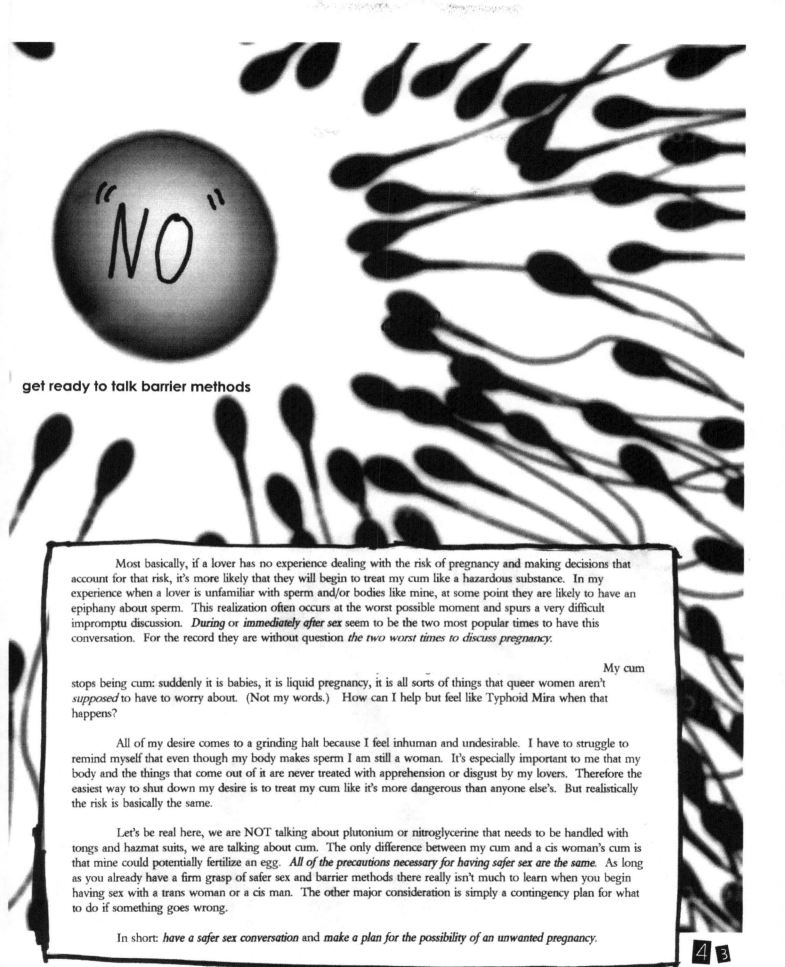

get ready to talk barrier methods

Most basically, if a lover has no experience dealing with the risk of pregnancy and making decisions that account for that risk, it's more likely that they will begin to treat my cum like a hazardous substance. In my experience when a lover is unfamiliar with sperm and/or bodies like mine, at some point they are likely to have an epiphany about sperm. This realization often occurs at the worst possible moment and spurs a very difficult impromptu discussion. *During* or *immediately after sex* seem to be the two most popular times to have this conversation. For the record they are without question *the two worst times to discuss pregnancy.*

My cum stops being cum: suddenly it is babies, it is liquid pregnancy, it is all sorts of things that queer women aren't *supposed* to have to worry about. (Not my words.) How can I help but feel like Typhoid Mira when that happens?

All of my desire comes to a grinding halt because I feel inhuman and undesirable. I have to struggle to remind myself that even though my body makes sperm I am still a woman. It's especially important to me that my body and the things that come out of it are never treated with apprehension or disgust by my lovers. Therefore the easiest way to shut down my desire is to treat my cum like it's more dangerous than anyone else's. But realistically the risk is basically the same.

Let's be real here, we are NOT talking about plutonium or nitroglycerine that needs to be handled with tongs and hazmat suits, we are talking about cum. The only difference between my cum and a cis woman's cum is that mine could potentially fertilize an egg. *All of the precautions necessary for having safer sex are the same.* As long as you already have a firm grasp of safer sex and barrier methods there really isn't much to learn when you begin having sex with a trans woman or a cis man. The other major consideration is simply a contingency plan for what to do if something goes wrong.

In short: *have a safer sex conversation* and *make a plan for the possibility of an unwanted pregnancy.*

If sperm, then what?

+Know how sperm work. Know how eggs work. Know how pregnancy occurs. Take everything seriously.

+No one knows their own sperm count. Please don't ask.

+Don't even discuss the odds of pregnancy, *assume they are 100%. Use barrier methods* and don't let sperm into your body.

+Don't treat semen like it's toxic waste, treat it like it is semen: a substance that can cause pregnancy and transfer certain kinds of diseases. Take it seriously but don't panic about its presence. Use barrier methods to prevent pregnancy.

+Use birth control as a supplement to barrier methods, not a replacement. You need condoms. If you want two layers of protection, consider birth control but understand what you're taking.

+Use spermicidal condoms and lube if you want, and unless anyone is allergic. Why the fuck not? (Unless someone is allergic. Then, that's why the fuck not.)

+*Don't treat hormone replacement therapy like baby insurance: it isn't.*

Date.
Mate.
Re-animate.

+*Talk about pregnancy* with sex partners, preferably sometime that is not immediately before, after, or during sex. *Make a plan.* Avoiding the subject is not going to help. Neither is talking about it incessantly. Make your plan and use prevention measures, aka *barrier methods and safer sex practices.*

+Whichever party can become pregnant is the person who needs to talk the most during discussions of pregnancy. What they want to do if and when a pregnancy occurs is what you will be doing, period.

+If you are a potential sperm donor, what you control is whether you have sex and whether *you* use safer sex practices. That's it. That's what you ultimately control. So if your partner doesn't want to use barrier methods or would prefer to carry a baby to term, it is your responsibility to know that and to plan accordingly. Your final prerogative is always to not have sex with that person.

+Either of you can always say no, and no means no at any time. Stop means stop. And 'get off of me' means 'get off of me.'

+*The best way to prevent a baby is to maintain safer sex practices: particularly, always use a barrier method.*

+Sperm can live outside a body for a while. They can also live inside someone else's body for a while. Don't let sperm into any orifice and stop the problem before it begins.

+If your partner is a trans woman, please don't call the sperm donor "the daddy" even as a joke. Don't.

+If you are concerned that you might be pregnant, get an over-the-counter pregnancy test first. They are very accurate . But pick up a second kit while you're at the store anyway. *It is customary* (at least where I am from) *for the sperm donor to pay for a pregnancy test.*

Sperm Meets Egg, Now What?

+See a doctor. Whatever you decide to do, see a doctor first. She can give you one last pregnancy test and tell you what your options are as well as direct you to resources. If at all possible, know who you are going to see and choose your care accordingly. You don't have to go to some asshole; find a good doctor who will treat you with respect.

+If you decide to have an abortion, that is first and foremost *your decision.* The sperm donor does not get a vote.

+If you are going to have an abortion, you will have to pay for it. This is one thing you should discuss with your sex partner as soon as possible: if this happens, who will pay for the abortion? Use your best judgment about what is fair, but *make a contingency plan.* I always keep money in reserve in case one of my sex partners wants or needs to have an abortion. If this is not possible for one or both parties, discuss that as well.

+If you decide to have a baby, that is your decision, and yours alone. The sperm donor does not get a vote. They are also legally responsible for expenses you incur during pregnancy, whether they want the baby or not. Make sure everyone is aware of this, but regardless, they are responsible for your love child.

+*Yes, you get to use the word "love child" if you decide to have the baby.*

+if you decide to carry the baby to term, the usefulness of this zine ends. Seek out a midwife, doctor, information, and as much support as you can find. Ask for help loudly and as often as necessary. And truly, best of luck to you.

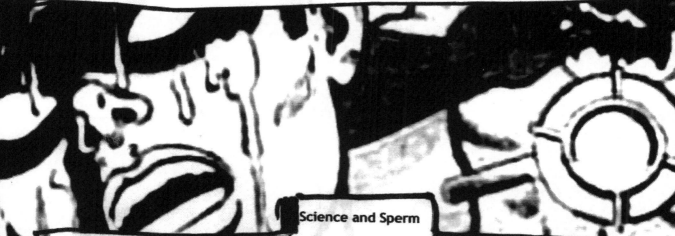

Science and Sperm

Science teaches us all sorts of interesting stuff about the human body. Consider the lowly sperm: inhabitant of the semen, denizen of the testicles, and occasional, overly-friendly explorer. Sperm are popularly known for looking uncomfortably like tadpoles, for congregating in ludicrously large numbers, and for causing people to get pregnant. Sperm cells are gametes, essentially smaller versions of their counterpart cells the eggs. But unlike ova, sperm cells are grown almost constantly, are very small, and number in the tens of millions. Sperm begin their lives in the interior of the testicles before moving outward to the epididymus where they pick up a tail. Equipped only with this whip-like tail and a dream, they are carried and nurtured in the seminal fluid that makes up the bulk of semen. Sperm are tenacious and relatively difficult to kill. They can survive for a short time outside the human body and still fertilize an egg; inside a human body they can survive for up to 5 days.

There are sperm in almost all semen, and in "pre-cum" as well.

There are millions of sperm in every drop of semen, and it only takes one to swim the distance to an egg and form a zygote. No matter what happens after that, things inevitably become more complicated and more expensive.

Sperm are haploid gametes.

45

Touch

Let me tell you about my *'no-zones'* – **I don't have any. I am the inverse of stone**.

I love being **touched** and groped everywhere on my body without exception. Human **touch** makes me feel good, and I crave it the way I crave sunlight or air or water. **Touch** makes me feel good about myself. It makes me feel present in my own body, which is how I prefer to feel.

So it makes me sad that since transitioning people touch me less frequently, lovers and friends included. I'm talking about everything from holding hands to friendly touches on the shoulder to vigorous rubbing of the upper thighs.

"No, I wasn't actually on edge, it's only that you're the first person to touch me today!" It sounds worse than it is. I am not a pathetic loner who no one touches, **but I do wonder where all the touch went and why it** went away

I think what's going on most of the time is that people – my friends included – are afraid that they're going to touch me in the wrong place or that it will seem disrespectful or something. Basically I think it's an attempt to be **polite**. Lovers do this too, generally more at first. I appreciate the sentiment, I guess? But it's **misdirected**, and if that politeness makes it all the way to sexy times **it becomes a real problem**.

A real PROBLEM.

What feels friendly and polite to me is touching me. **My body might feel different than what you're used to in subtle ways but really it's just my body, they're all a little different from each other.** <u>Trans is not catching,</u> and I don't usually smell.

I want you to touch me.

That's a hard thing to tell anyone and there is no convenient way to introduce the topic that I've found. But really, please stop being polite and start **touching** me more often, whether you're my friend or my lover. If you're my friend I'm not telling you to go out of your way, although if you did I wouldn't complain.

(it's not like I don't notice when you shy away from me even if you pretend not to. I can tell the difference. anyone can.)

Touch makes us feel human, it is what makes us feel welcome, and loved, and alive, and beautiful, and utterly *wanted* by the people who love us.

(I notice when my touch or my compliments give you that deer-in-the-headlights look, or you don't know how to respond. I notice when it takes you longer to hug me. I feel it when we share a bed as friends but your body is rigid. I don't say anything but I notice.

These things make me feel very sad.)

But if **we're fucking** then I <u>really</u> need you to **touch** me more. **Touch** me all the time. <u>*Do go out of your way*</u>, because most lovers I've had for the past three years who weren't other trans women have erred on the side of caution and left me feeling untouched, and untouchable. "Untouchable" is a rotten way to feel, especially when you're trying to fuck. Not to dwell on the negative but when someone doesn't touch me it also suggests pretty strongly that they don't find my body sexy. **I know that's not the case if we're fucking**, so what's up?! Put your hands on my body! Find the parts you like to touch, **then touch the shit out of them.** What feels sexy to me is being touched a lot, all over. *The more hands on my thighs, arms, chest, belly, legs, hands, shoulders, and back, the better.*

PLEASE stop BEING POLITE,
and if you are NOT being polite,
then STOP THAT TOO please.

I want you to
touch me, and really,
I am very touchable

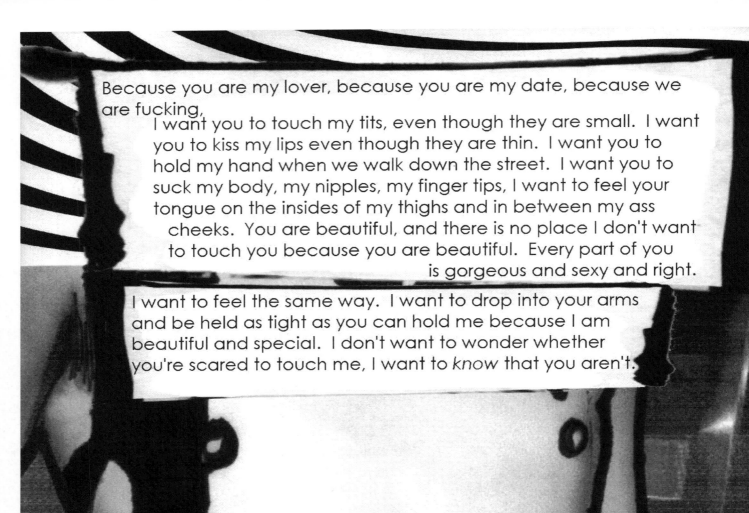

Because you are my lover, because you are my date, because we are fucking,
I want you to touch my tits, even though they are small. I want you to kiss my lips even though they are thin. I want you to hold my hand when we walk down the street. I want you to suck my body, my nipples, my finger tips, I want to feel your tongue on the insides of my thighs and in between my ass cheeks. You are beautiful, and there is no place I don't want to touch you because you are beautiful. Every part of you is gorgeous and sexy and right.

I want to feel the same way. I want to drop into your arms and be held as tight as you can hold me because I am beautiful and special. I don't want to wonder whether you're scared to touch me, I want to *know* that you aren't.

It can be hard to be touched sometimes, when I'm so used to no one touching me, but I want you to touch me. Even those rare times when I can't be touched, of course I wish that you could touch me and comfort me. And please know that if I'm not touching you, it doesn't mean that I don't want to. You are so very touchable, I want to touch you all the time.

(It gets to me sometimes, I admit. I start to wonder "am I touchable? Does anyone really want me?" And of course you do and I know that,

but I want you to show me anyway.)

this is what I know: I KNOW that my lovers want to touch me, I know that they see me as I am and think "that is the sexiest girl in the room, and she is my girl," and because I know that I am asking you to touch me.

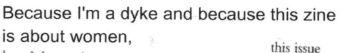

dyke

Because I'm a dyke and because this zine is about women, this issue doesn't have a lot to say about guys, although I am a fan. I identify as a trans dyke and most of my lust is reserved for women. I really love women, but I've run into some challenges dating cis women that I want to talk about.

One is non-matching equipment. There is a basic difference there, and it is frustrating to deal with lovers who are experienced except with bodies like mine. I get sick of being the first trans woman X person has slept with. I want my lovers to get my body and not treat it like a confusing math problem. I want them to have at least a rough idea of how I work, and that doesn't always happen.

I don't want to give you the wrong impression: most of the time having sex with cis women is great, just like having sex with trans women. Again, because I'm a big dyke, I fucking love women's bodies. I love pussy in any form.

I never did very well with straight girls.

When I started dating dykes, (and that happened well before I transitioned,) I discovered sex partners who were as interested in having interesting, challenging sex in a variety of ways as I was. That's one measure of good sex for me.

DON'T YOU HAVE ANY *INTEREST* IN BOYS, MIRA?

BOYS ARE A *DRAG!* BESIDES, THEY DON'T GO WITH MY OUTFITS

I *LIKE* AGNES TO HAVE FRIENDS OVER. SHE'S SO *SHY* WITH YOUNG PEOPLE!

AGNES ISN'T SHY ONCE YOU GET TO *KNOW* HER

Here's another: sex is good for me when the woman I'm having sex with treats me like a lady, (not a very ladylike one,) and dykes are good at that. Sex is great when the woman I'm fucking also has the skills to fuck all sorts of bodies, including women with penises, like me. Some of that comes from practice.

I know the difference between a beginner blowjob and a good one.

but on the other hand that's not always how I want someone to go down on me. **Often** I'm more interested in getting eaten out

One group of challenges that I've found has come from dating other femmes. (I'm a femme and I'm often interested in other femmes.) That is a challenge in itself, but being a trans dyke doesn't make it easier. I'm used to courting and dating femmes and feminine queer women; that doesn't feel at all like a problem or a challenge to me. But I've found that it is a challenge for some of the femmes I've dated.

Femme-femme desire is a hard thing to talk about. The problems don't show up where misogynist jokes would assume, but there are problems. I feel like, having dated plenty of femmes in my life, I have the advantage of experience. I know how to court and date other femmes. Sometimes they don't have much experience dating other femmes, and that creates frustration and problems.

As a femme, I function best when I am being actively courted and persued. Staying in and having sex is great, don't get me wrong, but one likes to be taken out and shown off. When you don't know *how* to do that for someone, sometimes you just *don't*. When that happens I feel frustrated. It's a dilemma and, sadly, the same factors that taught me to court are the ones that make me an unhelpful source of advice; I do *not* advise anyone do what I did and pretend to be a boy for several years.

Another frustration is the treatment my cis lovers sometimes get from other dykes. An acquaintance in Portland who has dated trans women put it this way: "Other dykes treat you like you won the jackpot if you're dating a trans guy, but they act like you don't know what you're missing if you're dating a trans woman." I don't see a lot of that unwanted pity when I am around, but I hear about it, and it frustrates the hell out of me. There is nothing – nothing – that a cis dyke or a trans guy knows about fucking women that I don't or can't know. Matching genitalia does not come with a guarantee that you are a good lover. It's actually curiosity and a hunger to learn as much about your lover's body as possible that makes good sex. Likewise I feel frustrated by the implication that I'm no fun to fuck. I am a good lay, if you basically know what you're doing. If you don't know the first thing about going down on me, that will be challenging. If you have never fucked someone in the ass, that will be even more challenging.

But that's the reason I like dating homos in the first place: we're usually up for a good challenge and are good at learning how to fuck people. That's part of who we are as a people. Other queer women constantly impress me by being more adaptable, resourceful, flexible, and devious than I might have guessed. And I generally guess in the direction of "resourceful pervert." By and large my lovers have recognized that they have, in fact, hit the jackpot.

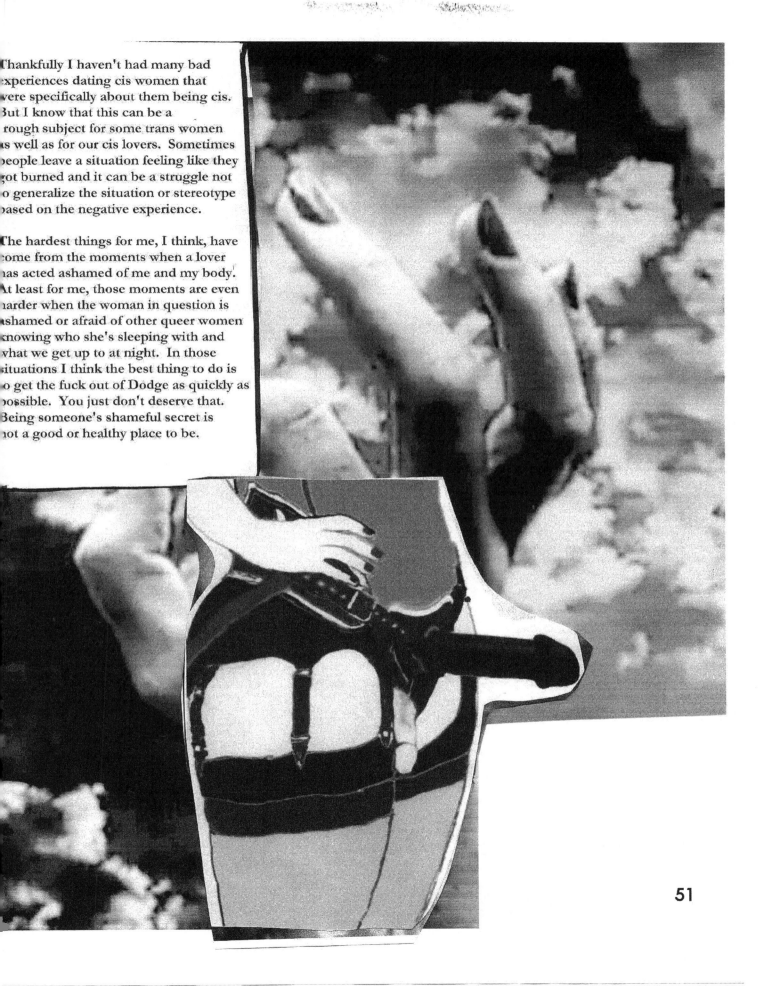

Thankfully I haven't had many bad experiences dating cis women that were specifically about them being cis. But I know that this can be a rough subject for some trans women as well as for our cis lovers. Sometimes people leave a situation feeling like they got burned and it can be a struggle not to generalize the situation or stereotype based on the negative experience.

The hardest things for me, I think, have come from the moments when a lover has acted ashamed of me and my body. At least for me, those moments are even harder when the woman in question is ashamed or afraid of other queer women knowing who she's sleeping with and what we get up to at night. In those situations I think the best thing to do is to get the fuck out of Dodge as quickly as possible. You just don't deserve that. Being someone's shameful secret is not a good or healthy place to be.

I wish my lovers would tell me more things they find sexy about me, because I live in a world that doesn't tell me much of anything positive about my body or my life. So I have started keeping track of compliments and saving them for when I need them. I also write down the things about other trans women that I find sexy.

I want to share some nice things I've written down about various lovers. Anonymously, of course.

Hey girl: I like your strong, smooth hands. You're a great kisser. Your smoky voice makes my cunt twitch. Your rosy cheeks are simply the cutest. I daydream about running my hands down your spine and playing with your asshole. Your thighs feel so good against my ass, strong and soft. Your eyes are so pretty that I want to grab you and kiss you every time that I see you. You are the smartest bitch I know, including myself. You have a way with words that makes talking to you on the street an exercise in restraint. You are sneaky in the best way. No one has ever made me feel as sexy as you did when you fucked me last night, and I really mean it. No one. Your energy is contagious.

"Being with her makes me feel like I'm 16 again; small, and naive, and horny, and like everything is possible"

You are very gentle at all the right times. Thank you for fucking me in the lounge with the door unlocked, the view of campus was really spectacular. You are so sweet, and so funny. You have really cute hair. I want to cum on your tits because they are so gorgeous. You're pretty. With your words and your body you make me feel like I'm the sexiest, smartest woman in the room no matter what. I want to lie around and listen to music with you all day. You are an amazing dancer.

"There aren't words. I've never met someone so gorgeous before in my whole life."

get effusive with me

I felt small and silly and embarrassed the first time I asked my lover to fuck me in what I named my cunts, and very very naked. Telling someone how to fuck you when you don't have the words is difficult, and you end up doing a lot of show and tell. All bodies are like that but some bodies have more names than others. For a long time I didn't even know what my body parts were called or the shape of the ones inside, I just knew how they felt and that my balls went up inside me. When I realized that I wanted someone to fuck me in this place that I had no name for I was excited, but also a little scared. On the one hand, I didn't really need to know what to call my parts in order to show one of my lovers what to do. When it came right down to it all I was asking for was for her to fuck a hole. On the other hand, saying what I wanted wasn't really the scary part.

The scary part, I think, was that I couldn't think of anything to compare with what I wanted. The way my cunts needed to get fucked was sort of like lots of things, but not exactly like anything, not even really close to anything I could think of. So I was a little afraid that I might get hurt and a little afraid that the person who was fucking me would get tired of trying to figure out my body on the fly. I got over it, partly by taking a bath.

It was the coldest part of Winter in Michigan and because I'm extremely sensitive to the cold, I needed to keep my apartment warm even though I bundled up indoors. My studio was old and drafty; ice collected in the closets and on the window sills. Since my utilities were included in my rent I decided to make the most of them. The steam heat was impossible to control so I had to choose between "on" and "off." When they were on the radiators were hot enough to melt plastic, but if I turned one off they might all go off, so they all stayed on. My studio apartment became a greenhouse. The only way to cool off was to open a screen-less window or two, and then it became a greenhouse with flurries. In the bathroom I had a claw foot bath tub all to myself and lots of very hot water; I don't think I ever took a shower in that apartment. Early in Winter I looped blue rope lights all around the unused rods and behind the translucent blue-floral shower curtain. When I closed the door and turned off the main light the room would fill with blue light and steam from the bath and flurries would drift through the window. The effect was serene and otherworldly, and probably a little trashy.

I think the two of us in that tub pressed against each other's bodies must have looked very sexy and very beautiful. We talked and fucked and ran more hot water and talked some more. Between us there wasn't much room for water. I told her about naming my cunts and then I asked if I could show her how to fuck them. Smiling, I faced her, put my feet up on either side of the tub, and then showed her where my cunts were. She pulled me out of the bath and into the bedroom, put me on the bed, and told me to show her again.

I know that she felt the tenderness and vulnerability of the moment, because she didn't make any jokes. Usually we joked all the time when we fucked, but we were both very quiet as I showed her how to press her fingers into me. What I remember most is her eyes, totally focused and intent. I could tell that she was trying to figure out the best way to fuck me right, and she was doing a fantastic job. My toes clenched; I forced myself to relax. Her fingers were precise, slow but deliberate as she determined where the best spots were. She smiled and told me to look at her. More and more of her fingers were inside me, pressing harder and harder as she fucked me with my own body and hers at the same time. My eyes rolled back into their sockets without any intentional instruction from my brain, which was slowly shutting down, preparing for something intense. An aching sensation pushed up my spine and back and all through my hips, spread out through me.

I drooled a little, my eyes went blurry and wet, my vocabulary evaporated. All I could do and all I wanted to do was be in myself, in my body, and feel what was happening to me. Everything except my body disappeared and all I wanted to do or think about was breathing. If there was a "me" in that moment she was at the base of my spine, certainly nowhere near my brain. I felt like I was uncoiling from inside. Sensations I had only guessed at before overloaded spinal reflexes and deep nerves. I tried to map the sensations ... I couldn't put words to the things I had felt or the place that had felt them, the sensations were simply visceral, they came from so far inside, right from the nerves. So many things are wound up inside of us in that part of the body, so many spinal nerves and organs, arteries, veins, the innervation of the gut; all of them felt alive, I felt alive.

sex story

53

Deep in the unclean bowels of the internet, nerds and terrible people make horrible inside jokes that spread and mutate and eventually become what we have learned to call "memes." At least 50% of memes are racist, sexist, homophobic, misogynist, or otherwise offensive; the rest involve cute animals. One of the most disgusting memes is the use of the word "trap" to describe trans women.

One of the most infamous memes on the internet began with Admiral Ackbar yelling "it's a trap!" during *Return of the Jedi*, which was funny because he's a squid and he was freaking out. Internet nerds *then* began using this scene, images of the squid-faced character, and especially the line "it's a trap!" to reference sexy images of transsexual women.

The basic structure of the 'joke' is to post a picture of a trans woman, wait for people to comment on how sexy she is, then reveal that she's trans, indicated by an image/quote of "it's a trap". This meme is very old and shows no signs of disappearing entirely. The word "trap" is now used by some assholes as a synonym for any person assigned male at birth who appears to be a woman; the "trap" they imagine is being lured into sexual desire for a woman who has a penis. There is also a latent assumption that all images of women invite their sexuality, and so a photo can be a "trap" whether the woman in it is masturbating or balancing her checkbook. To be labeled a "trap" is to be reduced to a sexual object that is taboo, and to be labeled a seductive deceiver who tricks heterosexual men out of their rather precarious sexuality simply by *being* seen.

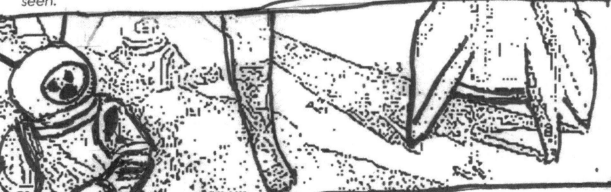

My favorite trap of all time is Myra Breckinridge from the novel *Myra Breckinridge*. I love this book dearly in spite of its many problems. Like lots of novels that feature transsexual characters the rep that this book usually gets is really awful: 'it totally misrepresents what it means to be a trans woman.' And that's true, it does. There are all sorts of things about being a trans woman that the novel gets completely wrong.

But Myra herself is not really a trans woman, she is a "trap": the personification of misogynist and transphobic fears of what a woman could be. Myra is not only a feminist and a transsexual, she is also an emasculating rapist who anally rapes a young, macho acting student named Rusty with a dildo.

I have to say, the chapter in which it takes place is pretty sexy. Myra slowly draws Rusty further and further into a medical sex scene that includes a prostate exam, anal massage, and a very deep "hernia exam" during which Myra penetrates Rusty with each of his own testicles. At the climax of the scene she binds his hands with gauze and rapes him on his knees with a fairly large dildo. Before he leaves to meet his waiting girlfriend, she makes him say "thank you, Miss Myra."

Note: This is a rape fantasy scene within what is basically an extended misogynist fantasy of a dangerous woman:

so fucking hot

(what makes the chapter interesting, and also difficult, and also compelling, is that you are reading a rape fantasy *within* the novel's fantasy of a woman who enjoys being a rapist. The whole of Myra Breckenridge is a kind of extended fantasy about violent women, so when Myra rapes Rusty, you're seeing a puppet show of misogynist fears. I find *the fear that motivates it* terribly sexy.)

Myra Breckinridge personifies one of the fears that motivate transphobia and misogyny, the fear of being sexually dominated by a feminine woman who secretly possesses and uses a phallus of her own, one that is larger and more powerful than a man's penis. "Myra Breckinridge" is the name of the "trap" incarnate: a woman that men fear and fantasize at the same time, the "New Woman whose astonishing history is a poignant amalgam of vulgar dreams and knife-sharp realities". Other women can and do fear her, too, but mostly because she is competition with whom they cannot

compete. The "trap" is not necessarily a transsexual, it's only important that she is a chick with a dick that you will only discover when she decides to fuck you with it. When she does, the act will strip you of your masculine pride and possibly drive you to homosexuality. Not only that, she is so seductive and so powerful that after she does these things to you, she will make you say "thank you, Miss Myra."

I'm not sure that "trap" is a word that I want to reclaim for myself, exactly. I reject all of the bullshit that goes with the word: the stereotype of trans women as deceivers who want to trick people into fucking us. The context in which I see that word makes reclaiming it even less appealing: it breaks my heart to occasionally stumble onto a discussion thread in which people are discussing pictures of my friends and whether they are men or women. I really have no wish to claim the words some use to justify such awful hateful behavior.

But I do think it is important that we don't rush to denounce the "trap" too forcefully or too broadly, because contained within that disgusting stereotype is a characterization of sexually powerful women that is worth holding onto. We should be careful not to reject that along with the phobic stereotypes. I feel similarly cautious about we trans women denouncing "fetishization." That denouncement often comes immediately before asserting that "we're not all sex workers" and a discussion of how gross "tranny chasers" are.

No, we're not all sex workers, *but some of us are*, and they are my friends and part of my community. No, it's not okay to fetishize parts of my body or my identity without my consent, *but if I give you my consent, then it is okay to objectify me.* And it is certainly okay to think and say that I am sexy, because I am, and it doesn't get said enough by the right people.

I could, and will, go on about why I think "tranny chasers" is a stupid way to name the problem of certain people acting creepy, but for now let's stick to the subject of trans women as sexual beings.

C ontained within the fear of the "trap" is the fear, a realistic fear, that women can be powerful and dangerous sexually. Phalluses are only <u>one</u> of the tools we have at our disposal to work our sex partners' bodies, but yes, some of us have penises and even more of us have cocks, and *plenty* of us want to fuck other people with or without them. Furthermore, our bodies are human bodies, and once you get us naked you will *see* human bodies. (<u>This</u> is the most generally applicable aspect of the fear of the "trap": <u>fear that a woman's body will not perfectly match one's expectations of what she *should* look like.</u>) And unlike simple images, women are subjects with desires of our own, plans of our own, schemes of our own.

We don't have to deny ourselves anything or prove that we deserve to be perverse

Enter the [illegible]

lush 'La Dolce Look'. for

CARAMELLA

Owning my own sexuality and my desires feels good and is part of being in possession of myself. I think we owe it to ourselves to live in that spirit, and not let others take it away from us by stigmatizing our sexuality or our bodies. I'm not a "trap," but I won't let my aversion to stereotypes of devious, deceptive shemales keep me from doing sexually what I damn well please. Do *I*, for example, want to (consensually) dominate younger men, tie them up, objectify their bodies, humiliate them, tease them, seduce them, and fuck their bodily orifices until they can barely breathe? Yes, I do. That is part of what I want. And when they leave, to say "thank you Miss Mira"

SSIONATA PINK

ALISSIMA

Almost none of my lovers have ever slept with a trans woman before me, so they have no basis for comparison, no experiential knowledge, and are therefore in almost uncharted territory. Most of the people I've slept with have been amazing lovers, and usually very experienced sexually. But most of that experience is from having sex with bodies that aren't like mine. Usually the women they've slept with have been cis, the men they've slept with are men, whether cis or trans.

When I've tried to talk about this with friends the response I get is largely silence, incomprehension, some sympathy. No one knows quite what to do or what might be helpful. Seek out partners who have experience with trans women? Sure, I can do that. And I can do my best to educate and affirm that it's okay to not know things.

But how can a potential lover find out more about having sex with me when there is literally almost *nothing* written about sex with trans women? Even something I considered only *partially* accurate or true would be helpful because it would give us something to start from, a common point of reference. Working without anything like this, I end up resorting to metaphor and show and tell. Those are not bad tools for education, but I know we can do better.

For instance, comparisons to how cis women and cis men like to fuck and get fucked are, to put it mildly, lacking a little something. Speaking only for myself, I don't feel sexy inviting comparisons to guys' dicks *too frequently*, and there are enough substantial differences in how I'm wired that I balk at telling someone to "fuck my cunts" without explanation.

"...No, not my asshole, my cunts."

"...No, not singular, plural."

"...(Here, I'll show you.)"

So sometimes one or more of us get frustrated or shut down because of terminology. And who can fault that? Using the wrong words for your sexiest parts is a total cold shower! Beyond the words themselves is the frustration that comes from an inadequate replacement or analogy. I feel this especially with euphemisms and neutralized terms.

I don't like calling any part of my body "my parts," "my bits," or especially "my junk." I mean really, **does anyone actually enjoy the word "junk"? My body isn't junk.** As far as you and I are concerned, anything you find on my body is gold-plated, diamond-studded magical pirate treasure, okay? My body parts are awesome

the 101

and are not junk. I have a narcissistic tattoo for a reason, and it's because I love my body.

modest person and I don't enjoy feeling like or acting like I'm ashamed of my body. Using those kinds of euphemisms fills me with a shame that I don't really feel *except* in those moments.

(Also… since we're on the subject, please don't ever use the word "treasure" while we're fucking. I'm sorry I brought it up. Thanks.)

It's no fun to give a quick "101" talk to a lover about how they should address my organs. I always feel like I should have made little name tags and prepared snacks. But I must say that it beats the alternative, which is to risk someone telling me something about my "dick" or "cock." No matter how my lovers identify or who they usually fuck, this problem just won't go away.

An example: I love everything to do with oral sex with almost any partner. However, I don't like receiving "blowjobs" because so often the scenario my lover constructs in their mind is that what they're sucking on is a cock. It's not. Even if it looks like you're sucking on a big ol' erect penis, I assure you that you are not sucking on a cock unless I say otherwise. Cock-sucking can be really hot, but on me it usually feels ridiculous, unwanted, and silly. It also seems to be the analogy that comes easiest to most of my lovers when they go down on me, and that's unfortunate.

What is even more unfortunate is that requests and demands to "eat my fucking pussy," "eat me out," or "suck my clit" are so rarely met with enthusiastic and knowledgeable responses. The worst reactions have been laughter, or being told that what I'm asking for is impossible, or being called a lez, or being told that "that" isn't sexy. First of all: *bullshit* and second of all: *fuck you.*

The fact remains that for me, good sex generally requires some explanation or even an anatomy lesson. Ultimately, these are fairly brief, and once we get started talking they're usually a lot more interesting and fun than I thought they would be. These days fucking me proper means getting a quick how-to on the inguinal canals and usually a little speech on soft penises. I imagine that lots of trans women, however you like to fuck, have similar speeches or lessons that you've learned to dole out quickly and efficiently, if perhaps just a little grudgingly.

Again... and again

The 101 is the conversation that you will inevitably have with your lover at some point, an educational (hopefully) talk about what they should and shouldn't do to make sure that you both have a good time and don't hurt each other. For trans women one important component of this conversation will almost always be what words to use for what parts of her body. Also which parts can be touched, how, and which parts are off-limits. All of this is pretty basic. Here are some ideas to *actually help you* develop your own 101 conversation and make sure that you are heard on the things you need to be heard on.

+ It's not a bad idea to take some time by yourself and think about what you want out of sex. Sit down at your computer or with a pen and paper and start writing: what feels good to you? What have some of your best experiences been so far? What would you like to do that you haven't? What would you like to do with this lover in particular? Most of us do this work in our heads anyway, putting it on paper simply helps. You can look over your ideas and get a sense of them as a real, tangible thing. You literally have a list of what you want to talk about, a sketch of what you want to do. *Naughty doodles are encouraged.*

+Find a comfortable place to talk to your lover besides your bedroom and have the conversation you need and want to have. The sooner you can do this the better.

It can be tempting to think to yourself that you don't need this, that you know what you want and are already in charge of your body and your situation. But don't kid yourself: the way bad situations happen is that someone gets overconfident and makes a mistake. That might be a simple language slip, it might be physically damaging if your lover doesn't know what they are doing, and either could have emotional reverberations in your life for a while afterward. The point is, don't get cocky about this part of communication. Build a consistent habit of talking about sex and you will ensure that the 101 happens, is worthwhile, and establishes your boundaries.

the 101

+ I find that it's helpful to say something early on about your lover doing some research on their own. Whether or not they are or feel knowledgeable about your body, it's a good idea to stay in the habit of treating each lover like an educational experience. There's stuff to learn from everyone and about everyone. Encouraging your lover to do their homework also helps you out when it comes to education and questions: they will have something to work with, even if it's not perfect. And they will not assume that you are the source of all information about trans women, which happens all too frequently.

+Talk about specific sex acts. Really roll up your sleeves and get into it. Can your lover fuck you in the ass, and if so, what feels good? What are your favorite toys? If your lover is a cis guy or another trans woman who wants to penetrate you with their own body, what safer sex tools will you use? What's your safe word? Is it okay to pee in your mouth? When does that feel good? Do you have allergies? Is fisting or fingering an option, and if so, in which holes or pockets or orifices should the hands go? Talk about verbal stuff, mental stuff, everything and anything as specifically as you feel is important. If something feels hard to talk about, it may be especially *important* to talk about. My trick in those situations is to close my eyes when I say the hard thing, but that may or not be helpful for you.

+How do you make the 101 easier? The same way you make anything easier: with practice. Practice. Write stuff down when you're not even seeing anyone and there are no prospects on the horizon. I don't think it's a bad idea to revisit past experiences, positive or negative, and think about what you might have done to make them even better, or figure out what you did right to make the good ones good.

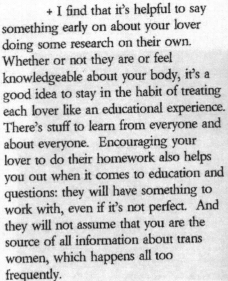

in which I say forbidden things

I found some pictures of myself as a boy today and I thought about how hot it must have been to put me in a dress and fuck me. In the picture I look like any cute young hipster boy you might see on the street. I'm wearing what was practically the uniform of my early twenties: a plain red t-shirt, a pair of tight jeans, black leather boots. I'm standing with my girlfriend in the driveway of her house after a weekend visit. My black hair is poking out from under my cap and a few curls spill down my forehead, contrasting sharply against my bright blue eyes and pale skin. Her hand is wrapped around my hips which I remember were covered in sweet little hickeys and aching, delicious bruises.

Almost nothing seems to me so intimately connected with sexuality and gender as drag. A host of queer theorists and writers have offered explanations for what drag is and what drag does, but few to none seem to notice that drag is sexy. So many try to explain what drag is, but that almost seems beside the point. Personally, I'm sick of hearing about drag as a transgressive gender performance, a capitulation to hegemonies of gender, a metaphor of queer identity, as a transformative experience or as a closeted one. Whose drag and under what circumstances? Why should we want it to be only one of these things? Drag performers are neither dupes nor demigods of gender, but we are often glorious.

I began playing dress up with girls when I was six, and kept it up all the way through my teens, stealing clothes and castoffs where I could. My parents moved us into the country where we had no friends, no girls next door, no way to escape. Every piece of clothing I could steal was precious to me. I would sneak into the bathroom late at night, lock the doors and experiment with makeup and clothes. That's all there was. That's what survival looked like.

It was vulnerable and it was tender and probably very sweet and a little sexy in spite of everything. I think back to who I was then and I wish so much that I could smile at myself, hold that girl in my arms and tell her she was perfect.

I was the smallest, slightest boy I knew, delicate and very, very pretty. Is it any wonder that when I started masturbating in my early teens my first object of desire was myself? I would slick back my blonde hair, apply black mascara to my long lashes and red lipstick to my thin, delicate lips, and simply look at myself. I would caress the tip of my penis gently with my fingertips, rock my hand back and forth across the velvety, shimmering skin. The ugly gold and white linoleum was my stage and the small sliding mirrors of the medicine cabinet were my audience. I would part my red lips and my thin fingers would glide over my chest and down my side, to my lower back and finally rest on my ass. My short red nails looked so pretty and so small resting on my thigh, my hip bones, my face, my knee, my arm. I was my own Lolita.

A while back a friend and I were talking and she mentioned the proliferation of trans guy porn, erotica, and art that have been produced in the last 10-15 years.

Although I love that it exists, I am envious of Trans Tiger Beat. I want that for me.
and I get sick of not seeing trans women making it happen

it's awesome to be taking charge of your own sexuality and body

It *is* very frustrating to feel left out of that, even moreso to feel like you don't have access to anything like it, could never do what they have done.

there are reasons why more trans women haven't stepped up and done more of it already, and for the most part those reasons *suck*. These include our Great National Fear of Fetishization, discomfort with sex at many levels for many people, a desire to not be like those "icky crossdressers" who take pictures of themselves in beige pantyhose and post them all over flickr, general body dysphoria, and by the numbers strong internal divisions in the general population of trans women.

We tend to cluster, divide, and avoid one another rather than work on common projects. This is especially true if and when we perceive major differences between our own way of being a trans woman and someone else's. We are sometimes overly picky about who we choose to relate to. Th straight trans women often don't wan anything to do with the queers and vic versa. But I want every trans woman I can get as friends and allies, if not collaborators, on many projects.

Anyway, my friend said to me that she was frustrated that she couldn't go out and take pictures of trans women and then display them in the Lexington. "That's already out there and it has a name, it's shemale porn."

Psst psst
Psst penis psst psst

Shémale

I considered that, and responded that I thought she was wrong. That if *she* made the images then they wouldn't be shemale porn. Look at all of the other kinds of porn that have been reappropriated from the earlier monopoly on porno-graphing held by straight white cis guys with cameras. We have learned that *part* of getting a handle on our own sexuality is to make our own pornography. Cis women, queers, people of color... all sorts of folks have already done this to one degree or another. But, it hasn't happened for trans women. Yet.

This is a project that we must take up, for so many reasons. One of the most important is that we need image control. As we know from Julia Serano's <u>Whipping Girl</u>, from our own experiences, and from the work of others, trans women currently have a huge image problem. The roots of this problem are extensive, but they include transphobia, they include misogyny, and they include stigma.

Shemales (and Other Friends)

We've just about got the name of the problem nailed, all of the stereotypes laid out in front of us, a sad collection of usual suspects: the shemale, the pathetic older transsexual, the tranny hooker, the murderous psychopath, the deceiver. When we are represented we are violently misrepresented and mischaracterized in certain ways that we're well familiar with. To fix the problem we need to represent *ourselves*, and we know that. There are obstacles. We know that too.

But one thing that we seem much less certain of is how to show ourselves being sexual without reducing or limiting who and what we are. I hear about this problem all the time. As I mentioned, we have become very good at blaming this problem on fetishization, at targeting fetishization and the stereotype that we are sex workers, and also at pinning this problem on others (chasers and whichever first-cousin-of-trans we don't like this week.) I am sick of hearing about it. I am ready to stop naming it and start rewriting the story.

A few years ago I found some old copies of the zine "Drag" in the archives of a university library. I took pictures of everything I could get my hands on for future study because I knew after 5 minutes with the collection that there was something there, a LOT of something.

In particular what I found that was worth unearthing was a spirit of sisterhood and cooperation between drag queens, transsexuals, and crossdressers manifested in articles that talked about our commonalities and shared experiences as well as our shared political struggles across communities. No matter how idealized or fictionalized this spirit was, I think it's worth looking back at fondly and remembering that we have been *trying* to change our image, *trying* to fight side by side, for as long as trans women have been calling ourselves by those words, and even before. That is part of

who we are and it is part of what we do. We don't just bicker, we also make strategic alliances, we also write our own stories, we also make our own media. We fight for what we want and what we need, sometimes with handbags and heels thrown at cops, sometimes simply by talking to each other.

We can be sexual without being *sexualized*. We really can. The key is simply to get there first, to talk out how we are sexual and to create our own images of what that looks like, of what we look like.

When I think about this project I often think back to feminism in the late 60s and 70s, because I think we're far enough behind that we need to borrow some of their tools. We are smaller, we are more spread out, than cis women have ever been. It is possible to be a trans woman and not regularly *see* other trans women, at all, ever. For that reason, I think it's probably a good idea to do some consciousness-raising. This seems to happen every time we talk to each other anyway, so why not make it a conscious effort? And since we're already talking about shared experiences, shared perceptions, shared bullshit, shared perspectives, we should also start talking about the parts of being a trans woman that are actually pretty great. I think we deserve that much and that we can give it to each other.

What better place to start than sex? Sex has been the ring in our collective noses: our sexuality, our sexy body parts, have all been used against us to portray us as monsters who are either too sexual or not sexual enough, usually both at the same time. The thing to do, then, is to get there first, to portray ourselves, and not only through negative definition, by saying what we are not. I will be the first to say that not talking can also be a strategy, but so far it isn't working very well. We really have to start saying *what* we do. We have to talk about our sexual practices, and the best and most important people to be talking to about that is each other.

It's the movie that never gets filmed

It's the story we won't tell

Some of the things we will say will necessarily be strategically limited. Sex is hard to talk about when you are us. And the ridiculous but nonetheless real burden of representation is going to feel heavy on our shoulders for a while. How do you say all that there is to be said? The answer is that you don't.

Say your own part. Take your own pictures. Draw your own art. Fuck the haters, and keep going. The rest will work itself out.

Start →
...2 new colors

First, courting is about making a gesture for someone else. Courting doesn't necessitate spending lots of money or being super formal or enforcing strict gender binaries. We're smarter than that. But it is about making gestures that basically say "I respect you." Whatever the specifics, let gestures of respect guide your actions.

Second, you don't have to take turns (but you can if you want to.) You can court someone on the same date that they are courting you. If you're not sure how try asking the person you're taking on the date to plan it out together. There's no rule that says you can't do this; there are no rules at all.

Courting ~~Disaster~~

When I was a young boy of 18 I had the good fortune to fall into the company of a woman with manners who liked to be courted. I really liked courting, and I got pretty good at it. I lit my dates' cigarettes, held doors, pulled out chairs and pushed them in, insisted on real dates, complimented freely, all the stuff that helps anyone have a good date and feel relaxed. But as a boy I often struggled to assert my desire to be courted. The two most common excuses – and they were excuses – I heard were "I don't know how" and "But I want to feel like a girl."

These days I would respond that it's not hard to learn, and that **courting someone doesn't make you any less a woman, it makes you more of one.**

Third, I've always found that asking a lover on **a real date is a good move.** It feels good to be asked. If they're not into it they will say so. Be explicit, be direct, lay out your intentions. Searching for a line? "I'd like to ask you out on a date." You're halfway there already.

Plunge everything on the new shimmering beiges

I really like being courted and yeah, for me part of being a girl is the assumption that people who are interested in me will court me a little, at least once in a while. It makes me feel sexy. And in return I'm more than happy to court back. I've found that a little can really go a long way toward making your date feel sexy no matter who they are.

Stop

On the other hand, **never taking your lover on a date can give them good cause to wonder just what it is you two are doing.** In my experience this is just as true for dating relationships as it is for purely sexual relationships. Even if you're both just in it for the fucking, it's good to show your appreciation by courting someone a little, by taking them out and showing them a good time as a gesture of care and appreciation.

Fourth, if you're on a date with someone, you are on a date with *that person.* The rest of the world, barring real emergencies, comes second. Plan dates so that this is practically possible: don't wander off. Don't – for example – leave your date at a dance in her fanciest dress waiting for you. That's bad form. Finally, try to remember that courting someone doesn't automatically assign you to a gender role *or* strip you of one. Boys can (and should) be courted; Girls can (and should) court.

When that doesn't happen, it generally makes me feel pretty gross. I feel suspicious that I'm being used for sex, but not in a hot way, more like a *convenient* way. Absence of courting also makes me wonder whether the person I'm fucking is ashamed to be seen with me, and that's a terrible suspicion to have. It feels gross to wonder if you're someone's dirty secret. (*Knowing* you are can be a different story, but I digress.)

Some of my lovers have been excellent at courting. Some have been absolutely awful at it. Courtship is delicate and complicated enough a topic that it deserves a full article at some date in the future, but for now please allow me to throw out a few general suggestions.

Take

it's the game every girl **Wins**

One of the more difficult obstacles to surmount when talking about sex is the intimidation factor. Far too many of us are scared to talk about sex in detailed specifics because we're not sure where we stand. The familiar anxiety of "they're all going to laugh at you" doesn't answer to reason, logic, or experience. When we're unsure of ourselves sexually it's easy to simply stop talking. After all, most of us probably *have* been shamed at some point for not knowing what one of our friends or lovers takes for the perfectly obvious.

It's like the old joke about how many hipsters it takes to screw in a lightbulb: "*You mean you don't know?*" Sex is where many of us feel the most exposed, the least knowledgeable, the most in need of teachers and advice and plenty of practice. Sex is one of the hardest subjects to admit one's ignorance about or lack of experience. It's also where many of us feel the most at home, the most confident, the most powerful, the sexiest, the most knowledgeable, the most experienced. And many of us feel both ways intensely and at the same time. There's no contradiction here, just the normal, everyday vertigo of experience and knowledge of a subject that's hard to talk about.

We can blame culture for a minute. American popular culture loves to tell us that sex is natural, good, and above all, normal. Also instinctual and obvious and frequent. We're meant to believe that aside from learning a few safety precautions your body just *knows* what to do with itself and someone else's body. And we're told that bad sex is more or less the opposite of this, totally boring and repetitive brand of "good sex": **bad sex is allegedly what happens when you try too hard** We're supposed to believe that bad sex is usually quite specific in terms of sexual acts, feels forced to one or more participants, is one-sided, or involves (god forbid) **effort** and **learning**

We're meant to laugh at two people trying to make sex work between them because, as any prime time soap opera will show you, sexual chemistry is instinctual. You just *know.* You're not supposed to need a manual. You're not supposed to need objects aside from your two bodies (no more, no less.) The music cues by itself, the lights go down, and the montage begins.

If you're reading this, odds are very good that you already know that this is complete horseshit. You probably know it so thoroughly that odds are good you wrote a paper about why it's horseshit at some point, potentially for a women's studies or gender studies class. You're probably pretty sex positive and don't buy into that kind of bullshit. Well, mostly.

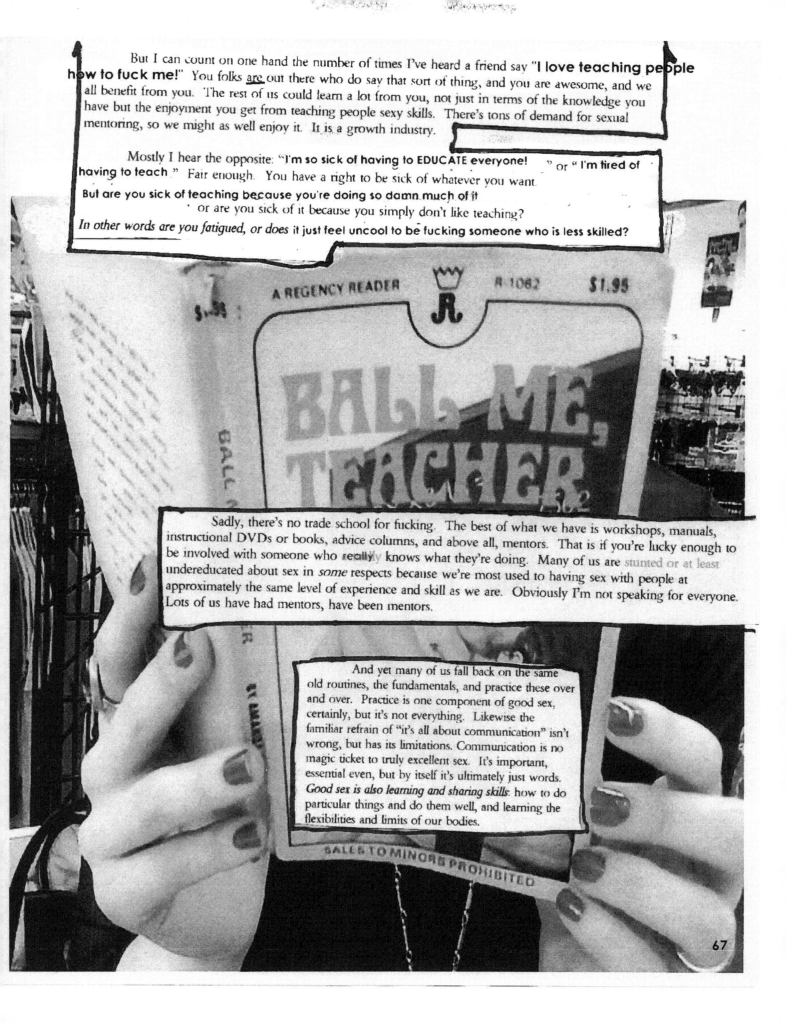

But I can count on one hand the number of times I've heard a friend say "**I love teaching people how to fuck me!**" You folks <u>are</u> out there who do say that sort of thing, and you are awesome, and we all benefit from you. The rest of us could learn a lot from you, not just in terms of the knowledge you have but the enjoyment you get from teaching people sexy skills. There's tons of demand for sexual mentoring, so we might as well enjoy it. It is a growth industry.

Mostly I hear the opposite: "**I'm so sick of having to EDUCATE everyone!** " or " **I'm tired of having to teach.**" Fair enough. You have a right to be sick of whatever you want.

But are you sick of teaching because you're doing so damn much of it
or are you sick of it because you simply don't like teaching?

In other words are you fatigued, or does it just feel uncool to be fucking someone who is less skilled?

A REGENCY READER   R-1062 $1.95

BALL ME, TEACHER

Sadly, there's no trade school for fucking. The best of what we have is workshops, manuals, instructional DVDs or books, advice columns, and above all, mentors. That is if you're lucky enough to be involved with someone who really knows what they're doing. Many of us are stunted or at least undereducated about sex in *some* respects because we're most used to having sex with people at approximately the same level of experience and skill as we are. Obviously I'm not speaking for everyone. Lots of us have had mentors, have been mentors.

And yet many of us fall back on the same old routines, the fundamentals, and practice these over and over. Practice is one component of good sex, certainly, but it's not everything. Likewise the familiar refrain of "it's all about communication" isn't wrong, but has its limitations. Communication is no magic ticket to truly excellent sex. It's important, essential even, but by itself it's ultimately just words. *Good sex is also learning and sharing skills*: how to do particular things and do them well, and learning the flexibilities and limits of our bodies.

SALES TO MINORS PROHIBITED

No, sadly there's no sex school except the one that we've created for ourselves in terms of self-education and experience. But that's no small thing. **The stuff we teach each other is knowledge.** We have built an institution in queer community of teaching each other how to fuck and learning as much as we can, at least about the things that directly interest us. . That sounds obvious and straightforward, right? We learn things from sex that make us better lovers or change the way we fuck. So take that seriously. *Sexual experience is an education in progress.* It informs how we have sex from one encounter to the next, from one partner to the next, and makes us better and better lovers. .

But are trans women actively doing these things, archiving our sexual experience and knowledge and passing it on, teaching each other how to fuck? not really .

It's all too easy to talk about the problems, the shared difficulties, the frustrating situations that we keep running into, and then commiserating about how hard it is to deal with these things. But it's more difficult, and more worthwhile I think, to start strategizing beyond even that, to start developing a shared knowledge base of what *does* work; what feels good and sexy and fun. To do that, to build a shared knowledge base, *we absolutely have to start by sharing information.* There is no way around this.

someone has to go first. Then, someone has to go second. And then we have to keep it going. We are going to have to step up and start talking about details. I'm talking about the specific details of what your body is doing when you are having sex.

The more suspicious responses I've gotten to this zine have also been the most reticent to disclose just these sorts of things. One person even accused me of trying to make them write erotica. as if I'm having trouble finding that) In fact what I'm hoping you'll share with me is very different: an account of *how* you have the best sex that you've had, not a story about it. *I want to share skills with you. It's as simple as that.* If we can focus our energy on communicating what works and what has felt really good, I think the end result will be better and better sex for us all and our lovers

The project of "Fucking Trans Women" is to create a documented, shared account of how we *like* to fuck and get fucked.

It is to create a shared, ongoing community resource in print. As I've already said, a cookbook that catalogues how we fuck, in any and every way.

That's the more difficult task, the more intimidating task: putting enough of yourself out there to be helpful to others. But it's also the more rewarding task because, if you put a little work in, you can end up making something that helps you understand what good sex is for you, something that helps remind you what an intensely sexy person you are and what an amazing lover you can be.

Look at it this way: we could talk shit all day and learn basically nothing, OR we could brainstorm. We could make a really helpful, useful, fun, entertaining, and sexy resource for our lovers, potential lovers, friends, and community. *Complaining about how often we have to educate people is simply not going to do anything to educate them,* or ourselves, or to help us find better ways to do that work. And our silence isn't doing us any favors whatsoever.

I want to acknowledge that talking about sex in this way is difficult. It's intimidating. Being the first person to put myself out there in this zine, to open myself up as much as I can, is risky, scary, gives me a feeling like vertigo. How much do I actually know? How much experience do I actually have, and how much will it speak to others? I've tried hard not to position myself as any kind of expert, but instead as an organizer and a sexual rabble-rouser

What I am asking for is a real, functional conversation about sex: what works. You can preface your own version of *what* works with as much qualification as you like. Feel free to preface everything with the reminder that your body is totally unique. And of course, it is. But you shouldn't be surprised when someone else finds what you have to say extremely helpful and applicable to their own body, which is *also* totally unique. *We are not nearly so unique as we'd like to think.*

More like RARE

Maybe the end result of reading this issue will be that you won't find much at all or maybe very little that's useful to you, but somebody has to start the conversation.

I've been asking former lovers, other trans women, friends, anyone I can think of, to pass along word about this project because what I've wanted to see is an outpouring of amazing, semi-secret stories and knowledge along the lines of "wait 'til you hear the sexy thing *I* did!" It took me a while to understand why I wasn't getting the responses I wanted from former lovers. They have their … reasons

For example:

+ "I don't want people to know how inexperienced I was."
+ "I don't want to go first."
+ "I'm not sure I have anything to say." *I got this especially from the people who've taught me the most about my own body.*

"I wrote something but it kind of stalled; I'll get back to it tomorrow, or maybe never. Whatever."

"Talking to other trans women about sex is depressing."

These are not good reasons to avoid talking to each other; there are NO good reasons to avoid talking to each other. If it's depressing to talk to other trans women about sex, it's because we're not doing enough of it and we're not talking about the right things: how to fuck and get fucked in ways that feel good to us and good for us.

This zine is your formal invitation to start.

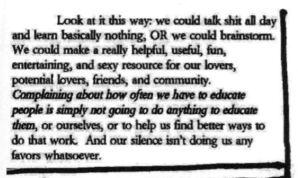

Why is this issue the "#0" issue? Why not #1? Well, it's *not* because I was inspired by comic books in the 1990s that started introducing #0 issues. Or maybe it is, a little bit. The Zero issue typically explains a lot of what is going on in a particular comic book for new readers without actually interrupting the main story. That part is certainly true of this issue: I wanted it to get conversation going by providing something to work off of, something to write back to and add to. It's also true that I didn't want this issue to be #1 so that contributors could have the chance to be in the first issue rather than the second. At a certain point, when I realized that there simply wasn't enough material in the submissions I'd gathered to make the zine I wanted, I decided I would do one whole issue myself to get the ball rolling. Now, I am not a humble person, but I did feel a little strange about "Issue #1" being completely composed of my own material. That didn't feel good to me. I felt like it would defeat the purpose of writing that whole first issue myself, because it would seem like this zine is *my* zine, my *personal* outlet and project.

This zine is *your* zine. I decided that "#0" might convey that a little more plainly.

This zine is also #0 because there isn't room for everything I want, because so much of it was done on the fly, and because I'm nervous about the parts of it that are not perfect. Literally *everything* in this issue is mine, including every mistake, omission, and problem. When something is not perfect, it is 100 my fault. All of my weaknesses show through: the bad "lightboxed" art created from photo collages, the images that were obviously borrowed under fair use, the notable absences.

The absences are what I worry about the most. The most frequent (and ignorant) criticism at the outset of this project was that it was impossible and/or offensive to create a "how to" zine about having sex with trans women because it would not be comprehensive, and/or it would try to say there was only one way of fucking trans women. That's a dumb criticism. The goal of this project has always been to *collect* stories and knowledge, not to authorize some and call those The Whole Story. That said, there will be absences especially at first. I ask you to bear with me and to contribute your own knowledge in order to fill in the gaps.

By The Numbers

Last Summer I created a short survey in anticipation of this zine, designed to collect information on what people were looking forward to the most *and* to get folks writing about their own experiences. The results were interesting, at times surprising, and at other times enormously frustrating. What I kept seeing was cis people and trans men, interested in dating and having sex with trans women but stymied by their own shyness and lack of information. Almost all of these people took pains to express that their desire was for people, not identities, or that they didn't want to limit their pool of sexual partners. Eventually they would get around to saying what they really wanted to say, which was that they were interested in trans women. **Finally.**

I also got lots of responses from trans women with very little or no sexual experience or with mostly bad sexual history. More than one woman said that she had never had a positive sexual experience. Sadly I had expected some of these responses, but each one seemed to catch me off-guard. A significantly overlapping group of trans women and women with trans experience or similar reported that they had major problems with their current genitalia and that this was a big part of why sex so far had not been enjoyable. These responses made me sad, but also angry for those women who hadn't been able to build an enjoyable sex life regardless, or find other things to do with their bodies. Whether they wanted bottom surgery or not, I wanted them to be having fun.

From the data I got a rough sense of several common problems. One seems to be that cis folks are shy about dating/having sex with trans women, and also about *naming* that desire and claiming it as valid. I think this is related to the fear of fetishizing someone else's body. That can be a bit of a ledge to walk, and that is a subject that deserves much more discussion at a future date. Likewise, I hope to see articles and work from trans women who have ideas about why sex is sometimes very difficult and not enjoyable, and some strategies for making it better. I have a suspicion that *some* responses of "I hate my penis" could lead into more complicated analyses of what experiences and dynamics make that so, beyond or in addition to dysphoria or disconnection from our bodies.

Finally, there were a few really amazing and encouraging results. I say a few but in truth the number I would call encouraging is somewhere around ¼ of the responses, about 20 responses in all. Trans women and our lovers reported excellent sex, new ideas, great experiences, fantastic love-making and fucking and debauchery. Many of the responses felt giddy as men and women described the fantastic sex they were enjoying regularly, sometimes to their own great surprise. These results say something.

They say that we are winning. They say that on our own and in small groups we have already started to strategize and think creatively about how we fuck and develop methods for getting around certain shared problems (by far the most common being communication and the 101 talk with new lovers.) Below are some *anonymous* selections from the survey that caught my attention.

"To have sex with me someone has to understand that they aren't going to get a "chick with a dick" in any way that that dick is doing any penetrating."

"It depends on who I'm with. Most people, I like to use my body mostly to please them. I often have a bit of trouble using my penis, because feeling "penetrative" is associated with unwanted feelings of masculinity, but if a girl wants me to penetrate her, I'll probably do it, as long as she's not a dick (pardon the pun) about using her dick as well (if appropriate). If woman is cis, I like strap-ons. I feel proud of my body when other people and myself like to look at it and it brings pleasure to me and my partner."

"I pretty much want to know about anything relevant or important to any partner I have, their body, their desire, the ways they want to be touched/not touched and any other needs around sex/intimacy/dating/talking etc. (And vice-versa, want any partners to be equally interested/engaged in me, my needs, my body, etc). Also, I think having specific information about safer sex, fluids, birth control in a zine - and maybe tips for how to have these conversations in a respectful way - is helpful."

"I hate giving the Trans 101. I attempt to make it as sexy as possible, but I really have trauma around having the discussion and answer the nervous questions about my body. I know it's necessary, but it is not sexy to me at all. I have had successful and sexy Trans 101's, but they are rare, and I dread it each and every time. Something I particularly hate is when people -- especially trans people or dykes -- stop mid-way through because my panties come down and they see I'm pre-op. This has happened a few times, and I'm starting to have a bit of a traumatic reaction about dropping trou with sexual partners, **and it's pissing me off.** Regular partners, or those who don't bat an eye at trans bodies AND understand my genderqueerity, really turn me on. I have found that, while I'm a very open and slutty person, I have this one wall that can only be overcome by those who have no qualms about my body (which either comes with regular sex or just that right sort of person), and it leaves me both turned on and very emotional."

"I think learning that a body part doesn't equal a gender was important. *Before my first trans lover and I ever kissed, I knew that in theory, and was able to be an ally and use the correct pronouns and all that - but when I was naked with someone, it was a different learning process. I figured it out eventually; I sort of just wish I had not immediately shared some of the things I was thinking with my girlfriend, though; a friend would have been better to talk to.*"

"...learning that it's okay for me to be attracted to trans women! While, as I said, I've had lovers all over the map, I do have somewhat of a tendency to go for a certain type of skinny smart femme slightly awkward trans woman. and I had some shame about that for a while- feeling like I was being a total fetishist or a creepy "transsenssual" person or something."

"I will admit I sometimes have recurrent twinges of shame- like "what if I'm being fucked up?"- but I remind myself that shame about desire is not usually a force for good politics. And also that people do have types, and if one of mine tends towards the trans women, that's not inherently any more fucked up than my sister's"

"I do remember the first time I fucked my first trans lover in the ass- and that was amazing because it was so hot and tender to feel her opening up to me like that. I remember with a much more casual date pinning her arms behind her head and how hot she got for that. I remember the first time with my long distance lover, how when she came she said "I'm sorry", and I didn't know what to say, and how different that is from the most recent time we slept together, how I fucked her a few times in a row, made her come hard and it was really good and she was definitely not apologizing. I remember one time I had my primary partner all tied up, and I was touching her and teasing her and eventually fucking her (I think, I can't even remember) and we were a little stoned and the whole time I was thinking about her cock as her clit and her testicles as labia... and it's all just different evolution from the same beginnings anyway."

"I blew an experiece with a non op lover ago because I didnt think I knew how to work with her body."

Boys and Other Gaps

You know who didn't make it into this issue in a big way? *Boys*. The reason boys don't appear much in this issue is that there isn't space. There are several mega-topics like "men" that also don't make a huge appearance, and I want to name a few of them because they are important, and should be incorporated into whatever meager beginning to the conversation I have created here.

Among these topics that are important, pressing, and extremely relevant are BDSM, race, different kinds of privilege, how bodily differences shape sexual experience, anal sex, gender play... the full list is extensive. About the time I hit 20 pages of single-spaced mini-essays and articles and instructions I realized that if I tried to touch on all of the things I thought were most important, I would have a book on my hands, not a zine.

...P in V fucking, trans/trans sex, the asshole,
...the prostate, tits, cbt,
post-op bodies, fisting...

So without surrendering responsibility for talking about all this stuff I want to invite you to help out by writing and drawing what you know and contributing to further issues. I will do my best to keep conversation going and expanding.

there wasn't time or room to be comprehensive

and I wanted to save my favorite stuff for later issues

...there's so much to talk about.

submissions

"Fucking Trans Women" is an ongoing publication seeking submissions: art, writing, How-To guides, diagrams, instructions, and other creative products.

If you would like to submit your own materials, please email:

If you are interested in participating in this zine in other capacities such as design or distribution, *please email*, we'd love the help

Future issues will also feature a letters section and a Q&A feature. Letters and questions may be submitted by email to the same address:

submit@fuckingtranswomen.com

"Fucking Trans Women" is a zine for trans women & our lovers, whatever their identities. If you have something to say, say it! If you have something to add or contribute to this project, **submit it!** We want you just as much as you want us.

This is your project.
This is your zine.

NEXT ISSUE

+ Anal Sex

+ Trans/Trans Sex

+ BDSM

+ Your submissions

+Did I mention anal sex?!

AND MUCH MORE...

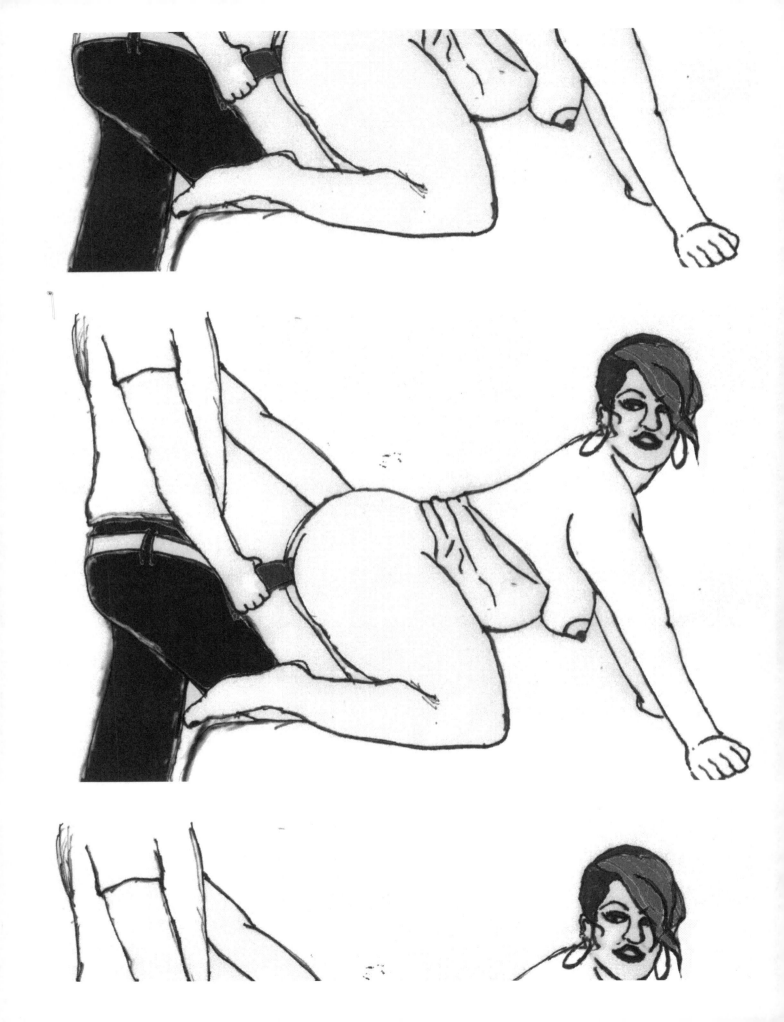

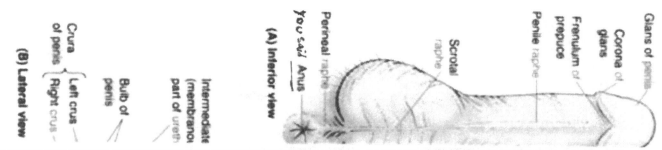

Miranda Darling Bellwether is a 28-year-old trans dyke and student. Mira is a femme, a queer, a dork, a cocksucker, and lots of other things. Her interests include the history of medicine, the 1920s, literature, masculinity as cultural narrative, homos, conversation, and the history of eugenics and racism. Mira reads comic books and can't take the cold.

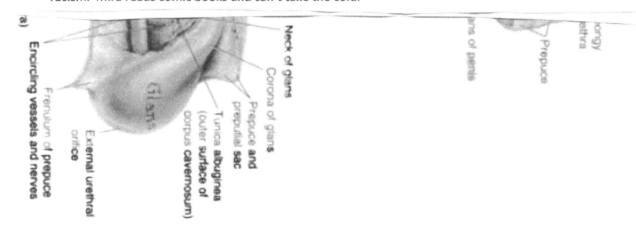

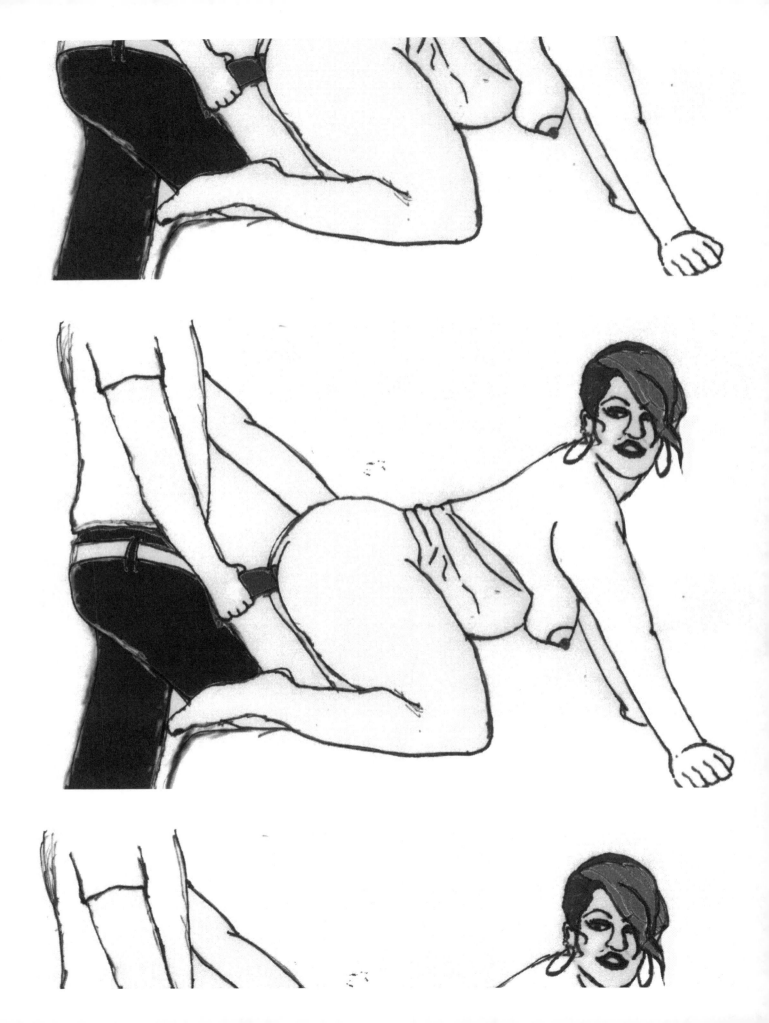

Made in the USA
Middletown, DE
05 June 2020